HOW I SURVIVED
FOUR NIGHTS ON THE ICE

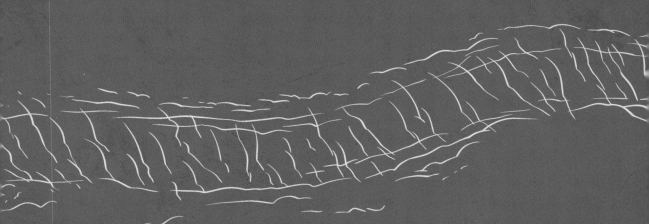

INHABIT
MEDIA

PUBLISHED BY INHABIT MEDIA INC.
WWW.INHABITMEDIA.COM

INHABIT MEDIA INC. (IQALUIT) P.O. BOX 11125, IQALUIT, NUNAVUT, X0A 1H0
(TORONTO) 191 EGLINTON AVENUE EAST, SUITE 301, TORONTO, ONTARIO, M4P 1K1

EDITORS: NEIL CHRISTOPHER, KELLY WARD, AND MONICA ITTUSARDJUAT
ART DIRECTOR: DANNY CHRISTOPHER AND ASTRID ARIJANTO
DESIGNER: SAM TSE

WE ACKNOWLEDGE THE SUPPORT OF THE CANADA COUNCIL FOR THE ARTS FOR OUR PUBLISHING PROGRAM.

THIS PROJECT WAS MADE POSSIBLE IN PART BY THE GOVERNMENT OF CANADA.
CE PROJET A ÉTÉ RENDU POSSIBLE EN PARTIE GRÂCE AU GOUVERNEMENT DU CANADA.

ISBN: 978-1-77227-426-4

PRINTED IN CANADA

Canada

Canada Council for the Arts
Conseil des Arts du Canada

HOW I SURVIVED

FOUR NIGHTS ON THE ICE

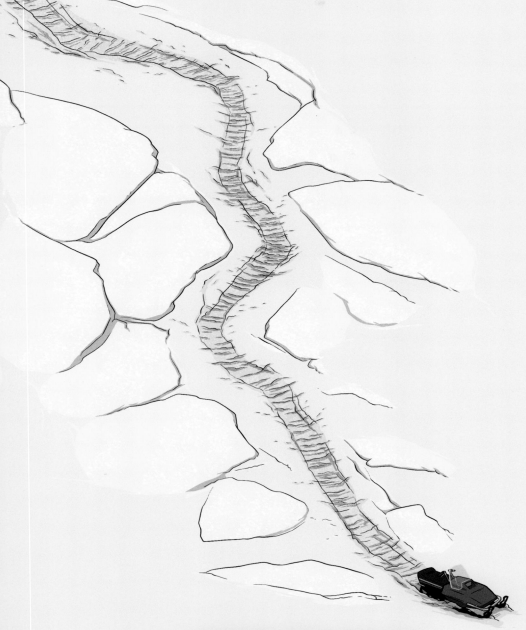

BY SERAPIO ITTUSARDJUAT

ILLUSTRATED BY MATTHEW K. HODDY

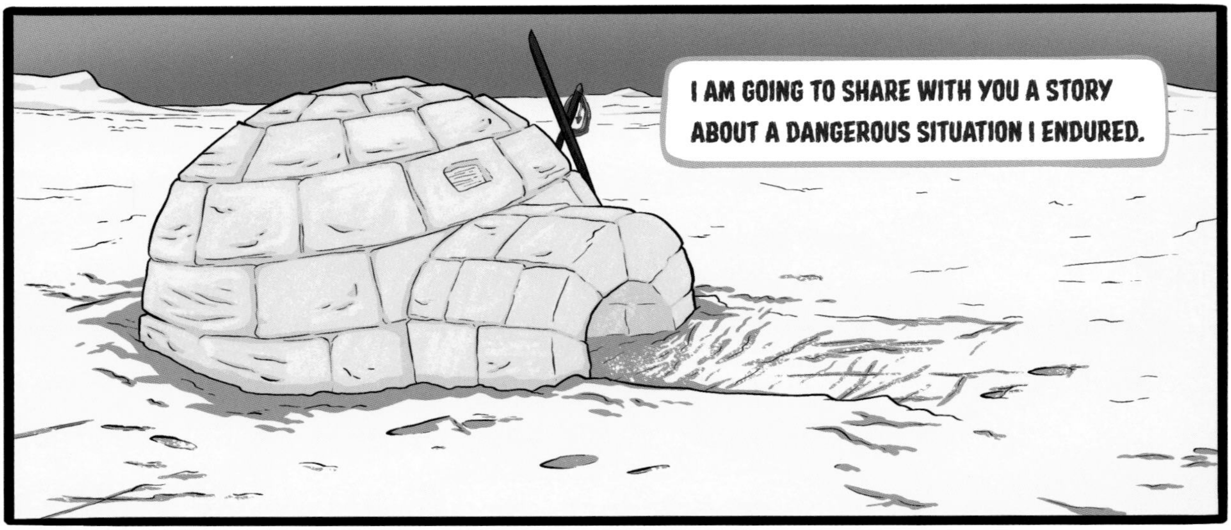
I AM GOING TO SHARE WITH YOU A STORY ABOUT A DANGEROUS SITUATION I ENDURED.

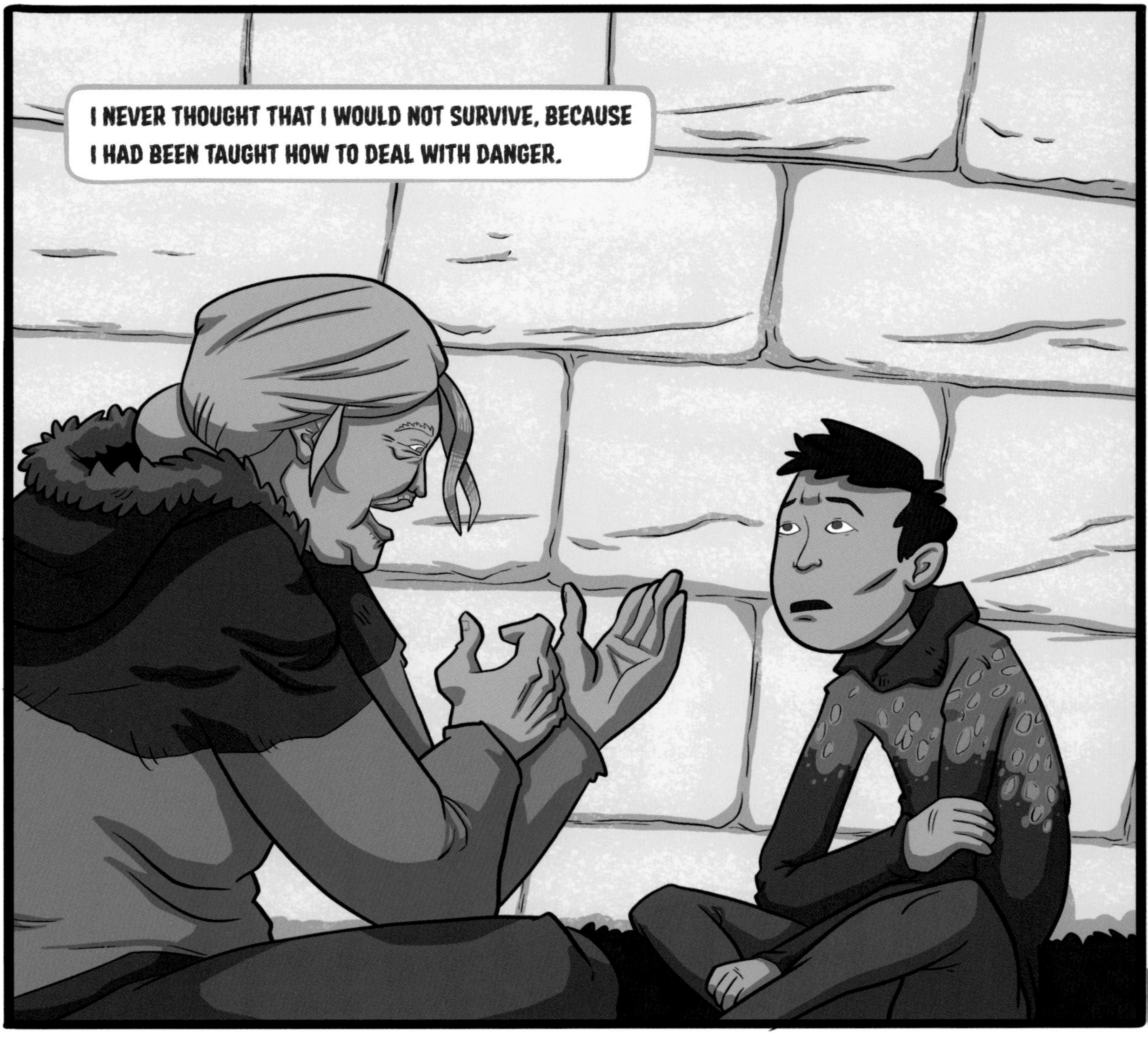
I NEVER THOUGHT THAT I WOULD NOT SURVIVE, BECAUSE I HAD BEEN TAUGHT HOW TO DEAL WITH DANGER.

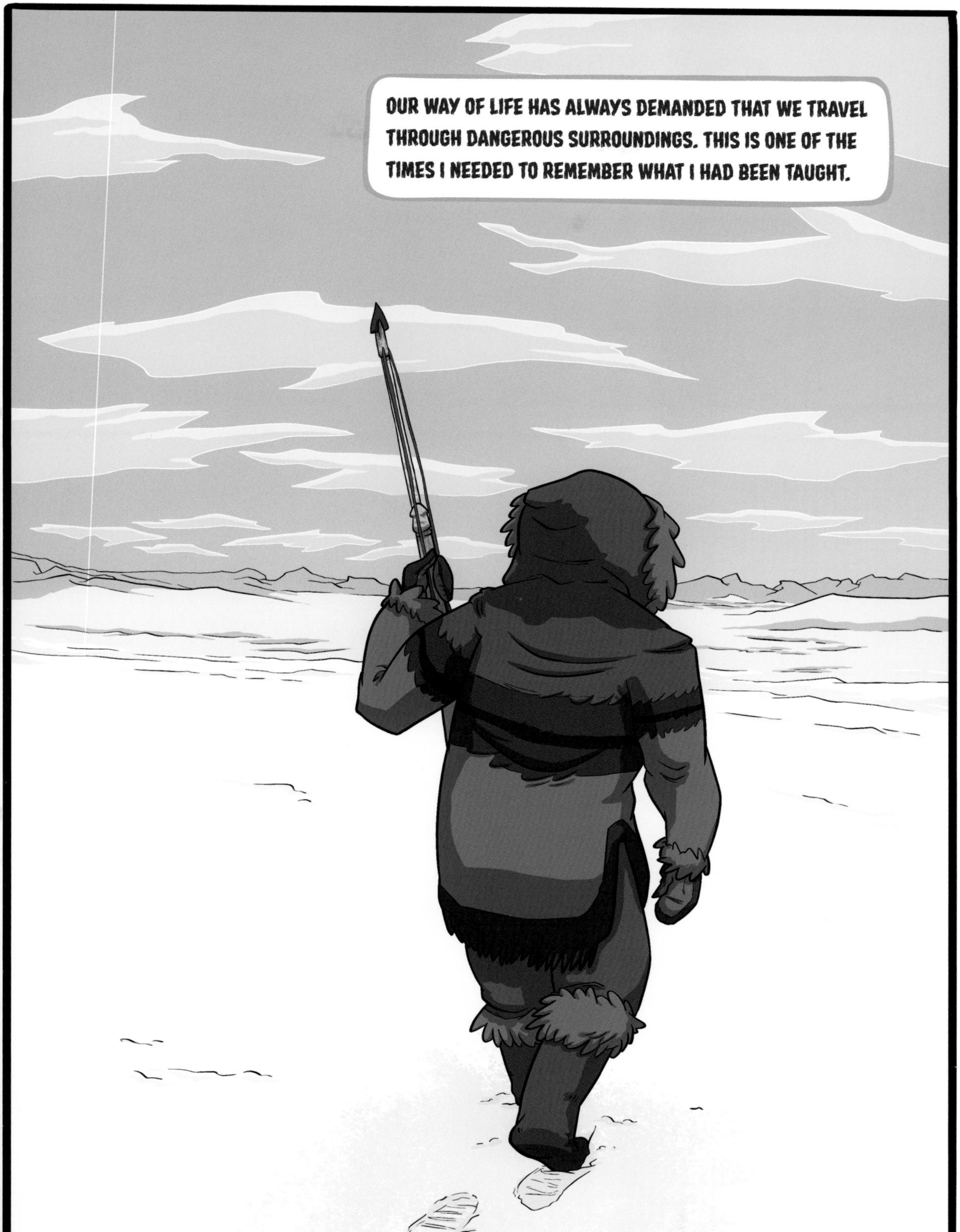
OUR WAY OF LIFE HAS ALWAYS DEMANDED THAT WE TRAVEL THROUGH DANGEROUS SURROUNDINGS. THIS IS ONE OF THE TIMES I NEEDED TO REMEMBER WHAT I HAD BEEN TAUGHT.

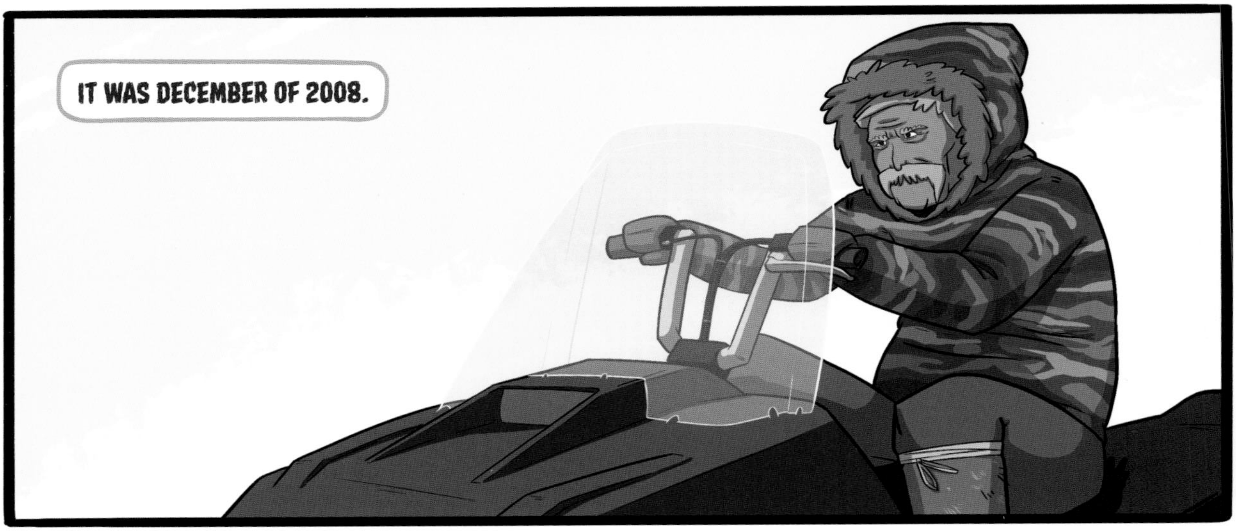
IT WAS DECEMBER OF 2008.

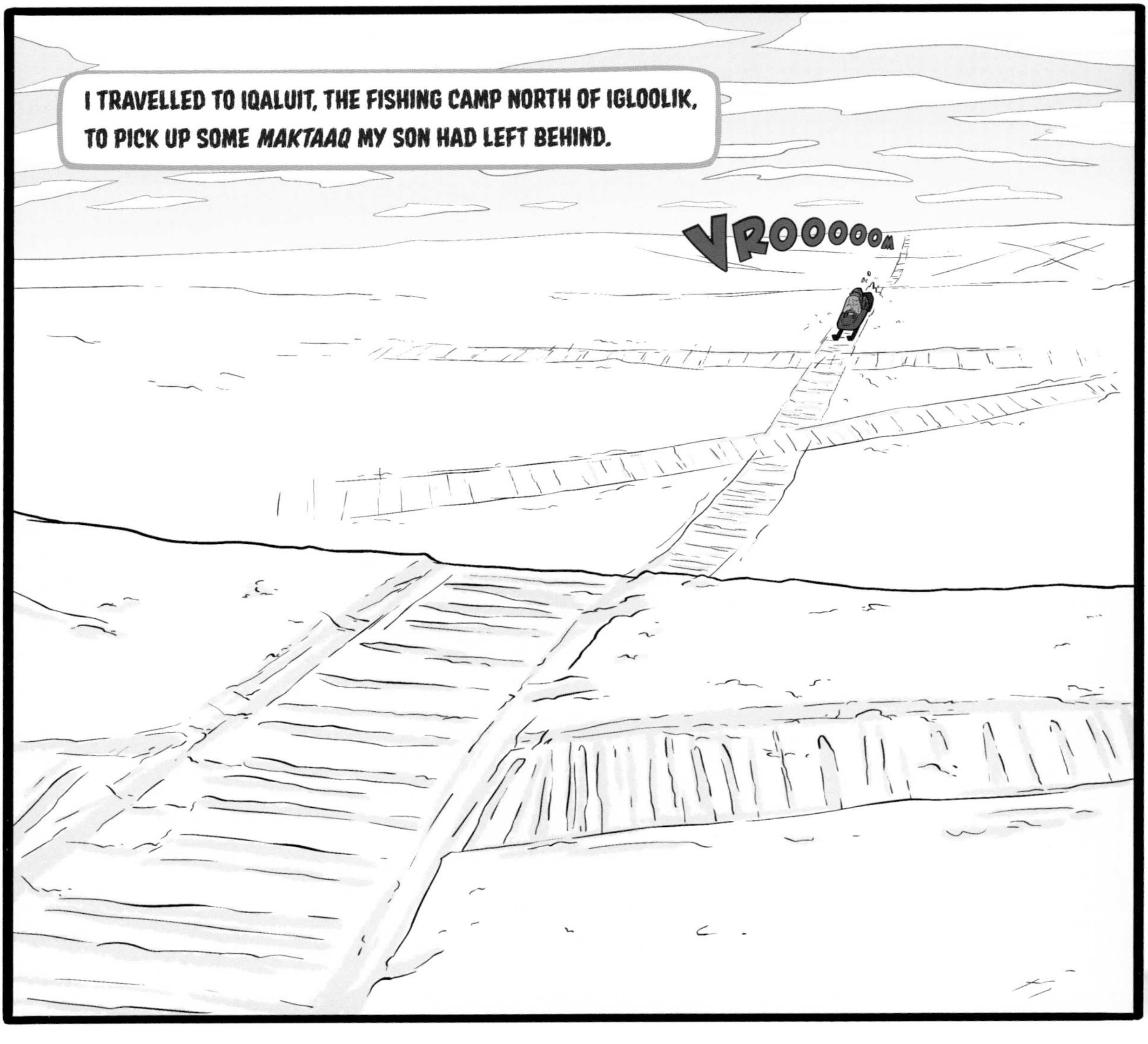
I TRAVELLED TO IQALUIT, THE FISHING CAMP NORTH OF IGLOOLIK, TO PICK UP SOME *MAKTAAQ* MY SON HAD LEFT BEHIND.
VROOOOOOM

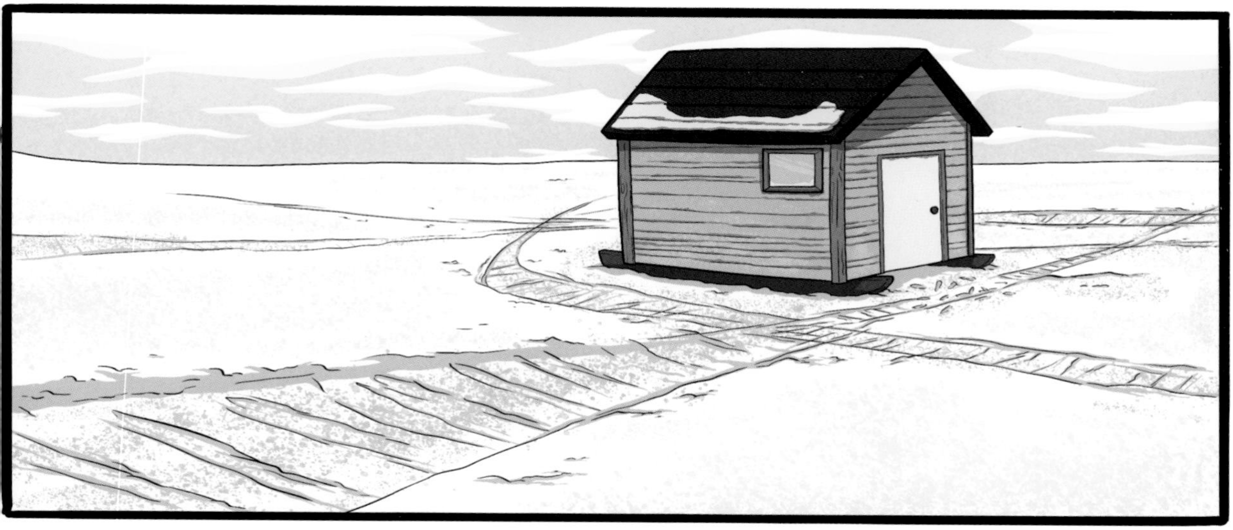

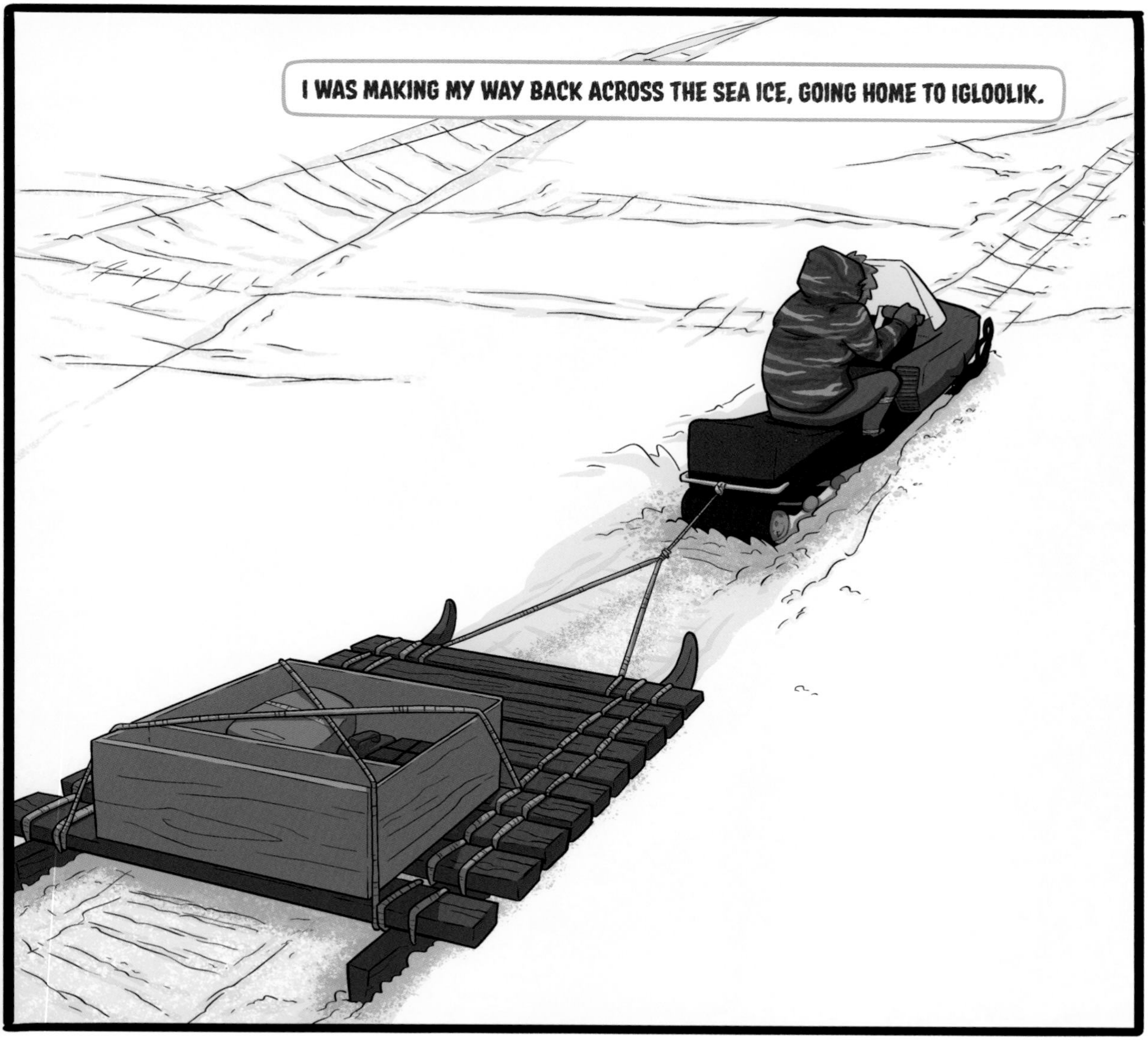
I WAS MAKING MY WAY BACK ACROSS THE SEA ICE, GOING HOME TO IGLOOLIK.

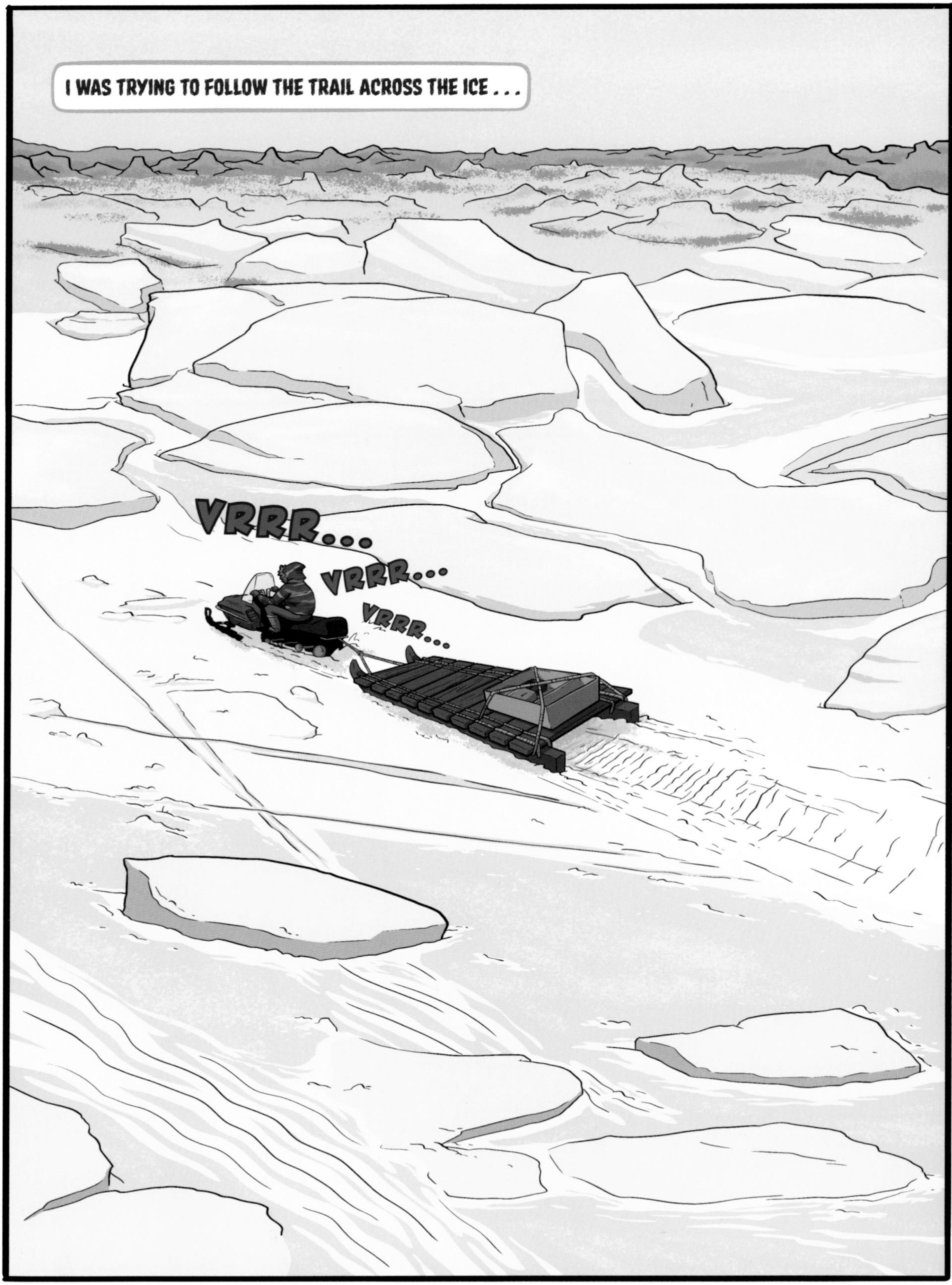
I WAS TRYING TO FOLLOW THE TRAIL ACROSS THE ICE . . .
VRRR...
VRRR...
VRRR...

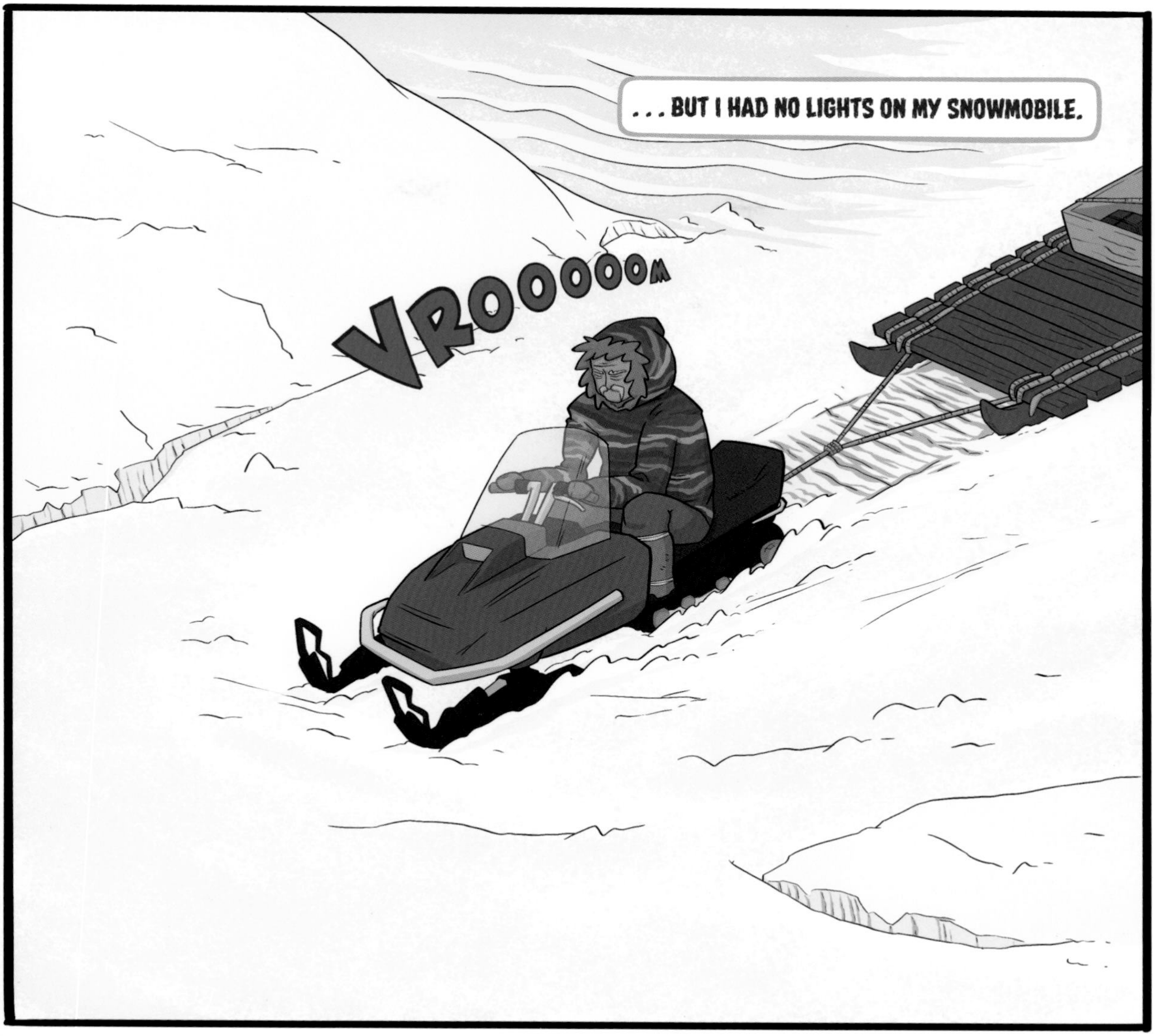
. . . BUT I HAD NO LIGHTS ON MY SNOWMOBILE.
VROOOOOM

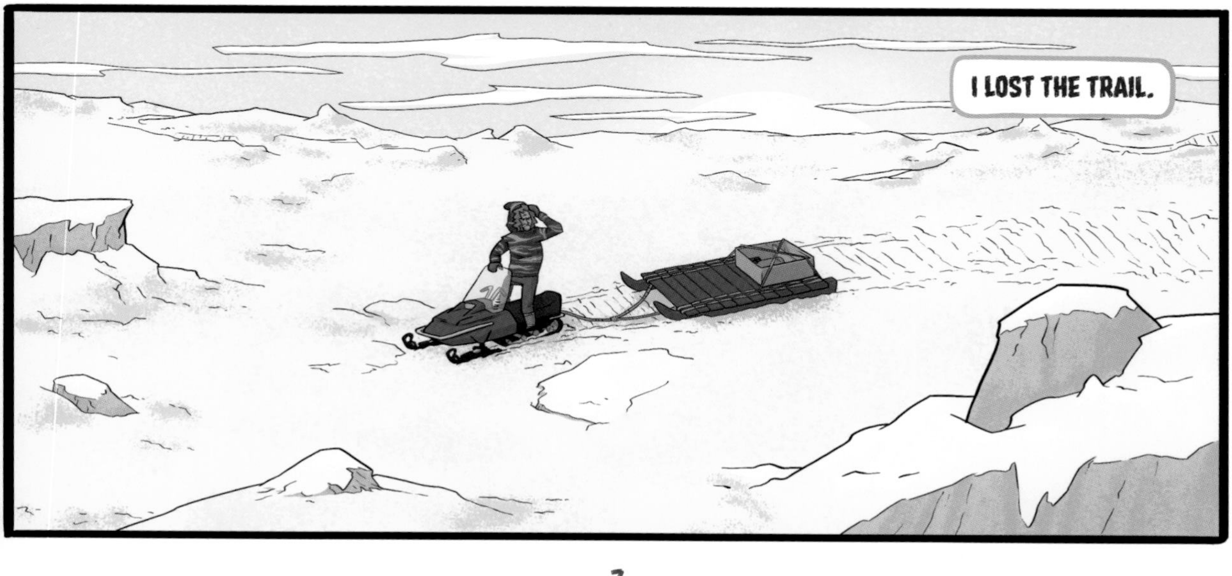
I LOST THE TRAIL.

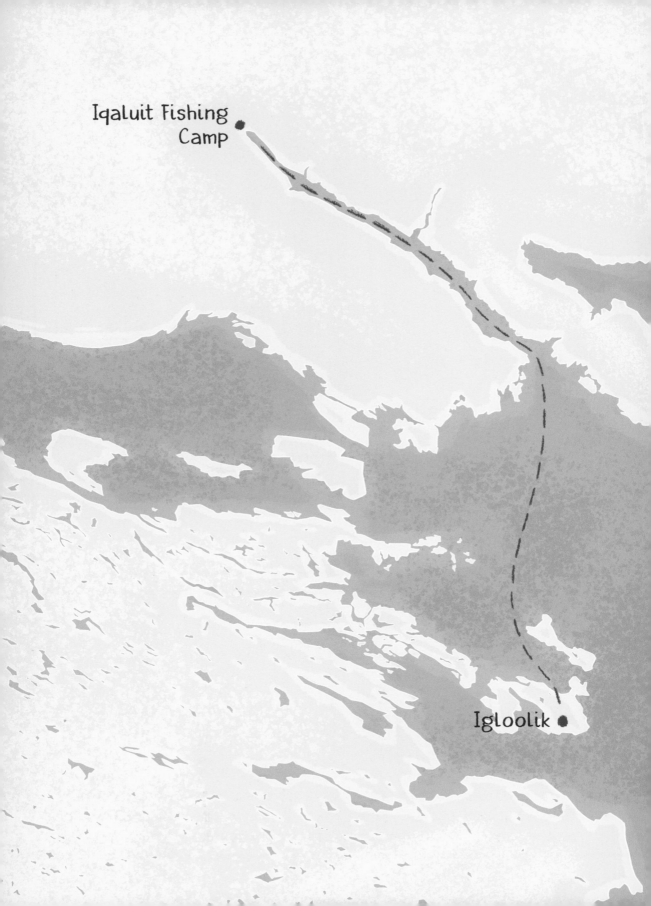

Iqaluit Fishing
Camp

Igloolik

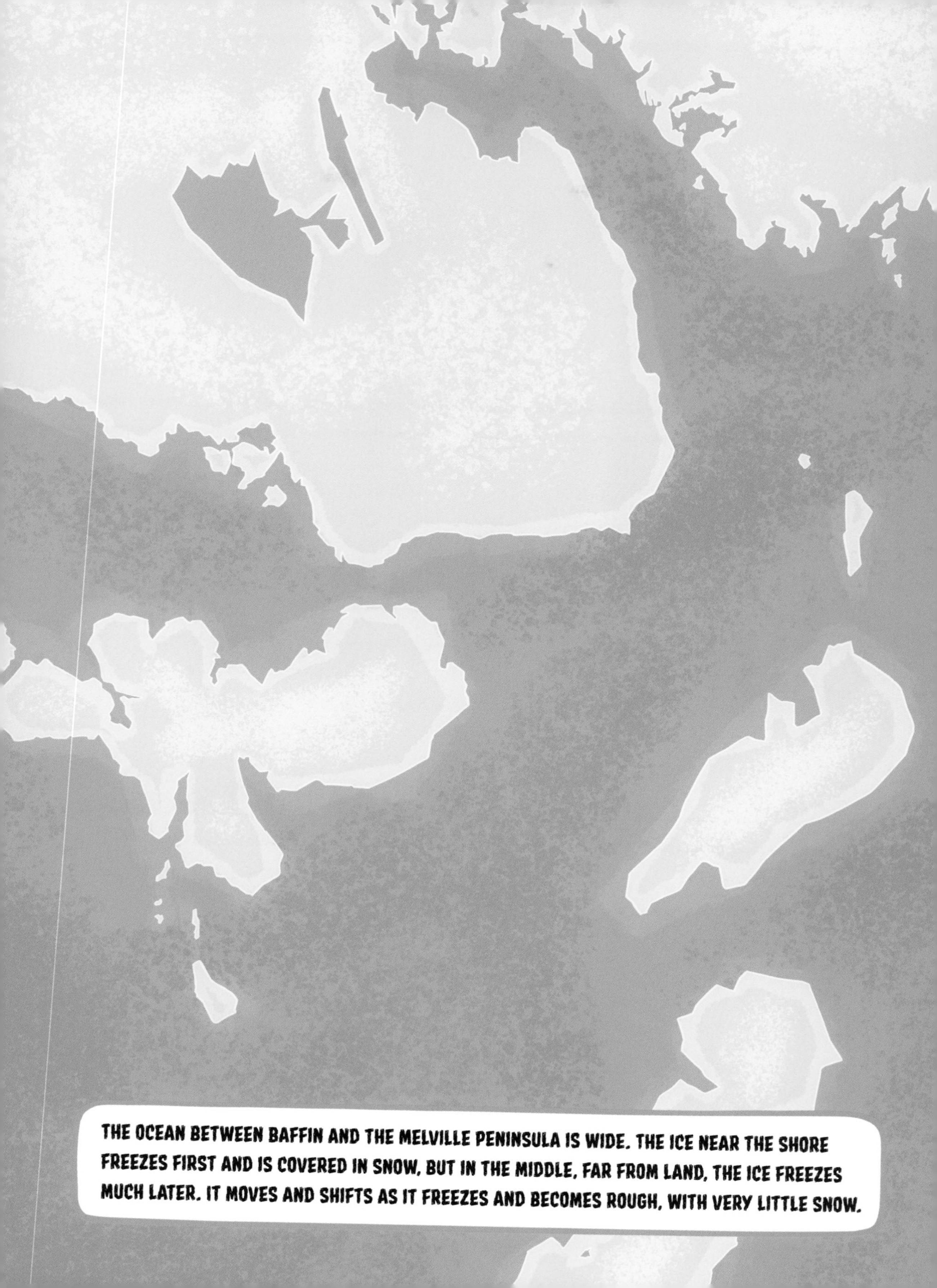

THE OCEAN BETWEEN BAFFIN AND THE MELVILLE PENINSULA IS WIDE. THE ICE NEAR THE SHORE FREEZES FIRST AND IS COVERED IN SNOW, BUT IN THE MIDDLE, FAR FROM LAND, THE ICE FREEZES MUCH LATER. IT MOVES AND SHIFTS AS IT FREEZES AND BECOMES ROUGH, WITH VERY LITTLE SNOW.

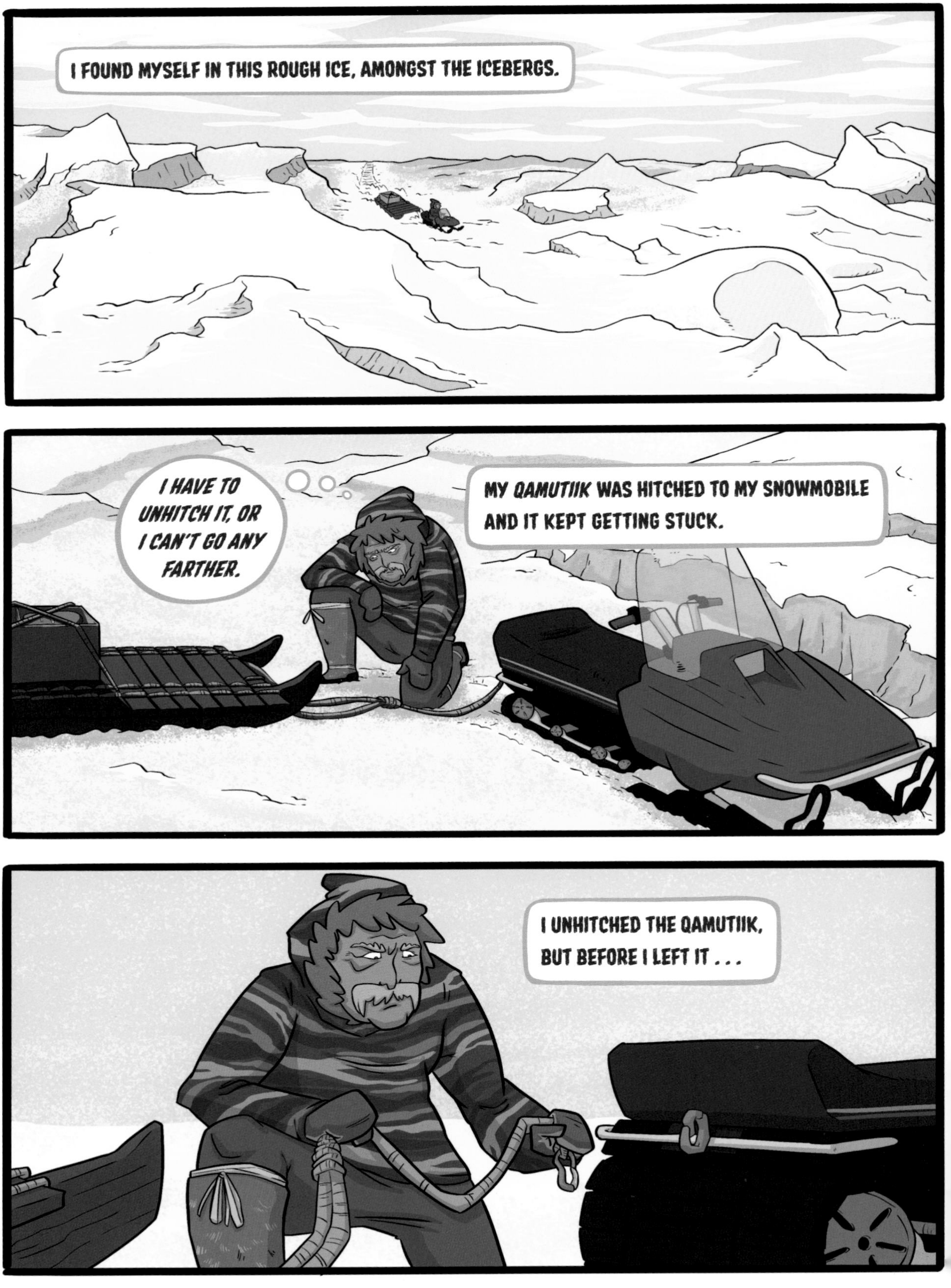
I FOUND MYSELF IN THIS ROUGH ICE, AMONGST THE ICEBERGS.
I HAVE TO UNHITCH IT, OR I CAN'T GO ANY FARTHER.
MY QAMUTIIK WAS HITCHED TO MY SNOWMOBILE AND IT KEPT GETTING STUCK.
I UNHITCHED THE QAMUTIIK, BUT BEFORE I LEFT IT . . .

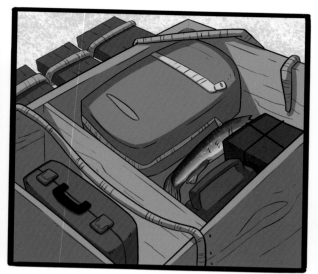

. . . I ATE THE FOOD THAT I HAD BROUGHT WITH ME.

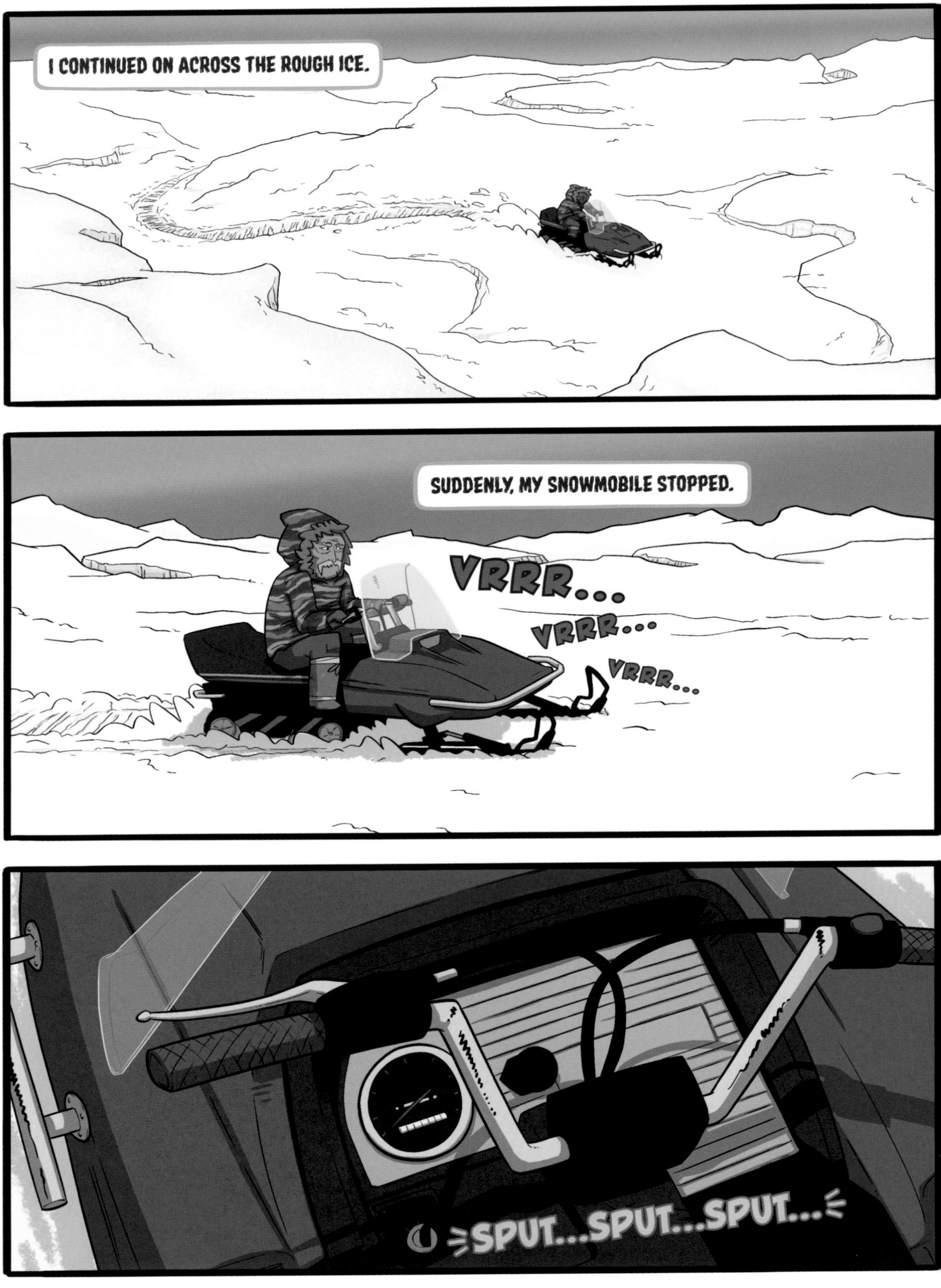
I CONTINUED ON ACROSS THE ROUGH ICE.
SUDDENLY, MY SNOWMOBILE STOPPED.
VRRR...
VRRR...
VRRR...
SPUT...SPUT...SPUT...

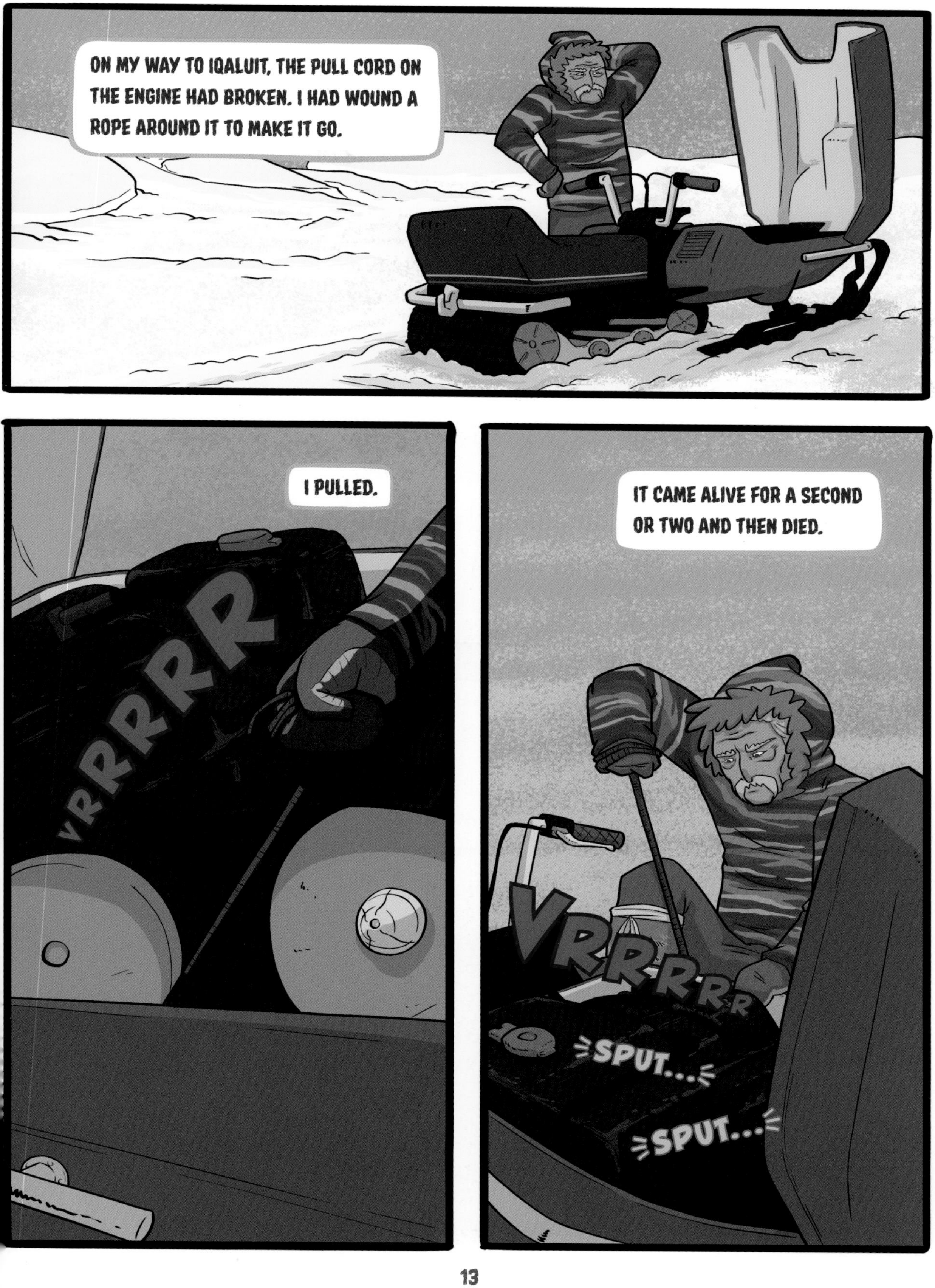
ON MY WAY TO IQALUIT, THE PULL CORD ON THE ENGINE HAD BROKEN. I HAD WOUND A ROPE AROUND IT TO MAKE IT GO.
I PULLED.
VRRRRRR
IT CAME ALIVE FOR A SECOND OR TWO AND THEN DIED.
VRRRRRR
SPUT...
SPUT...

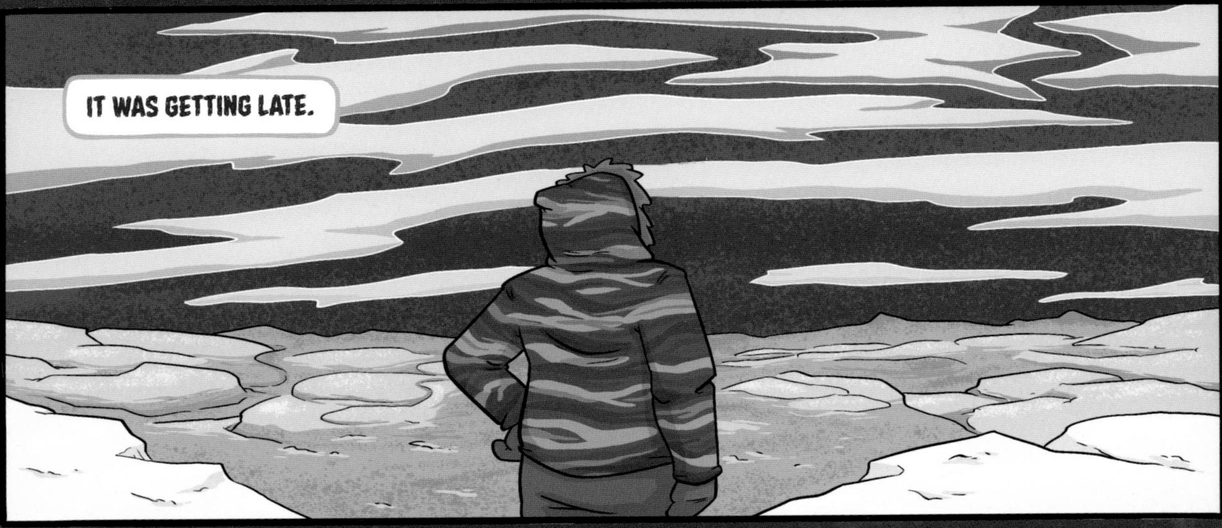
IT WAS GETTING LATE.

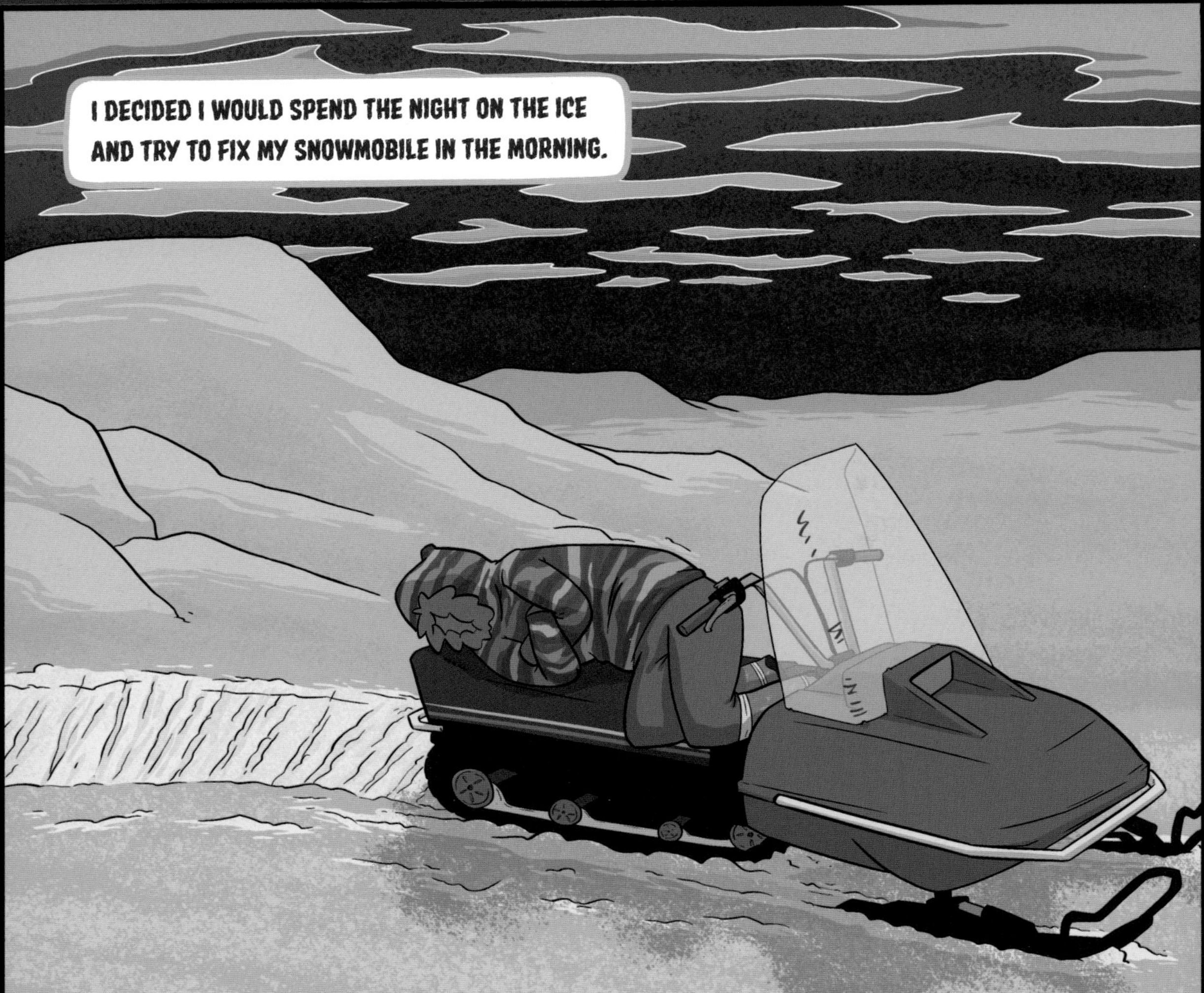
I DECIDED I WOULD SPEND THE NIGHT ON THE ICE AND TRY TO FIX MY SNOWMOBILE IN THE MORNING.

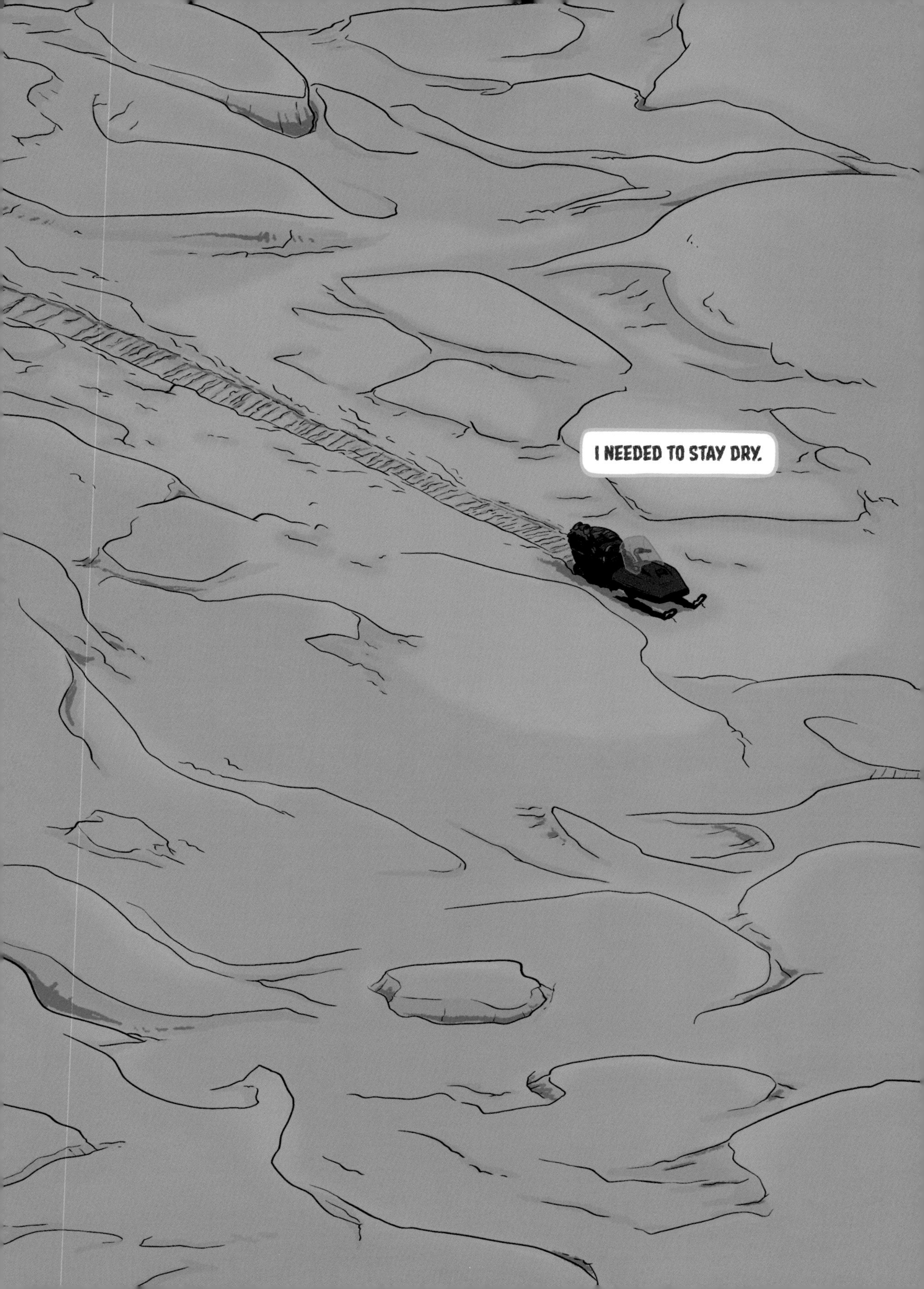
I NEEDED TO STAY DRY.

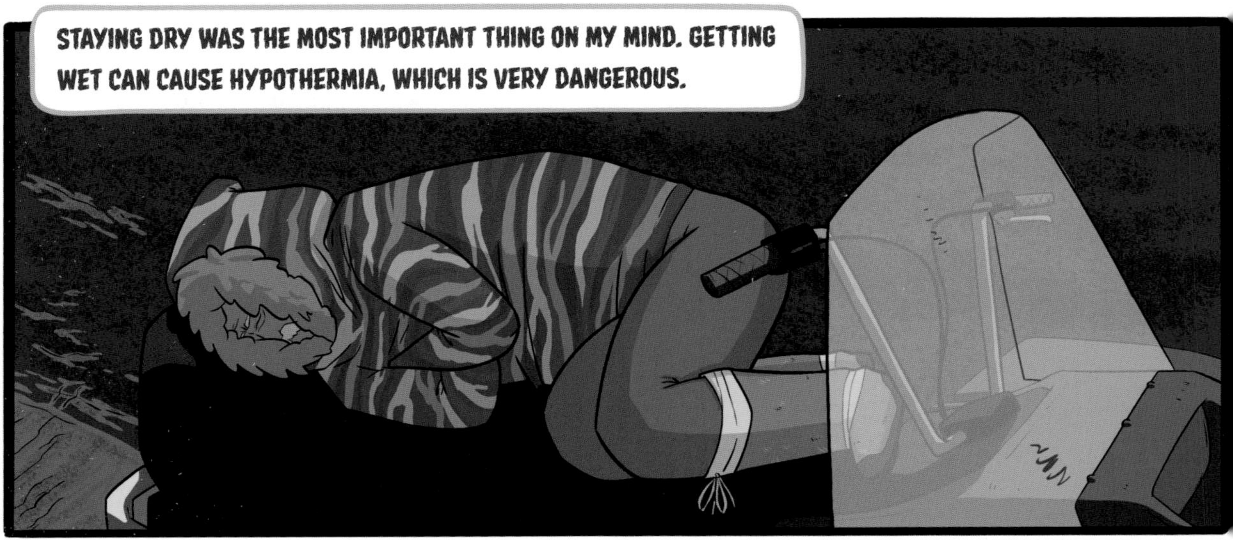
STAYING DRY WAS THE MOST IMPORTANT THING ON MY MIND. GETTING WET CAN CAUSE HYPOTHERMIA, WHICH IS VERY DANGEROUS.

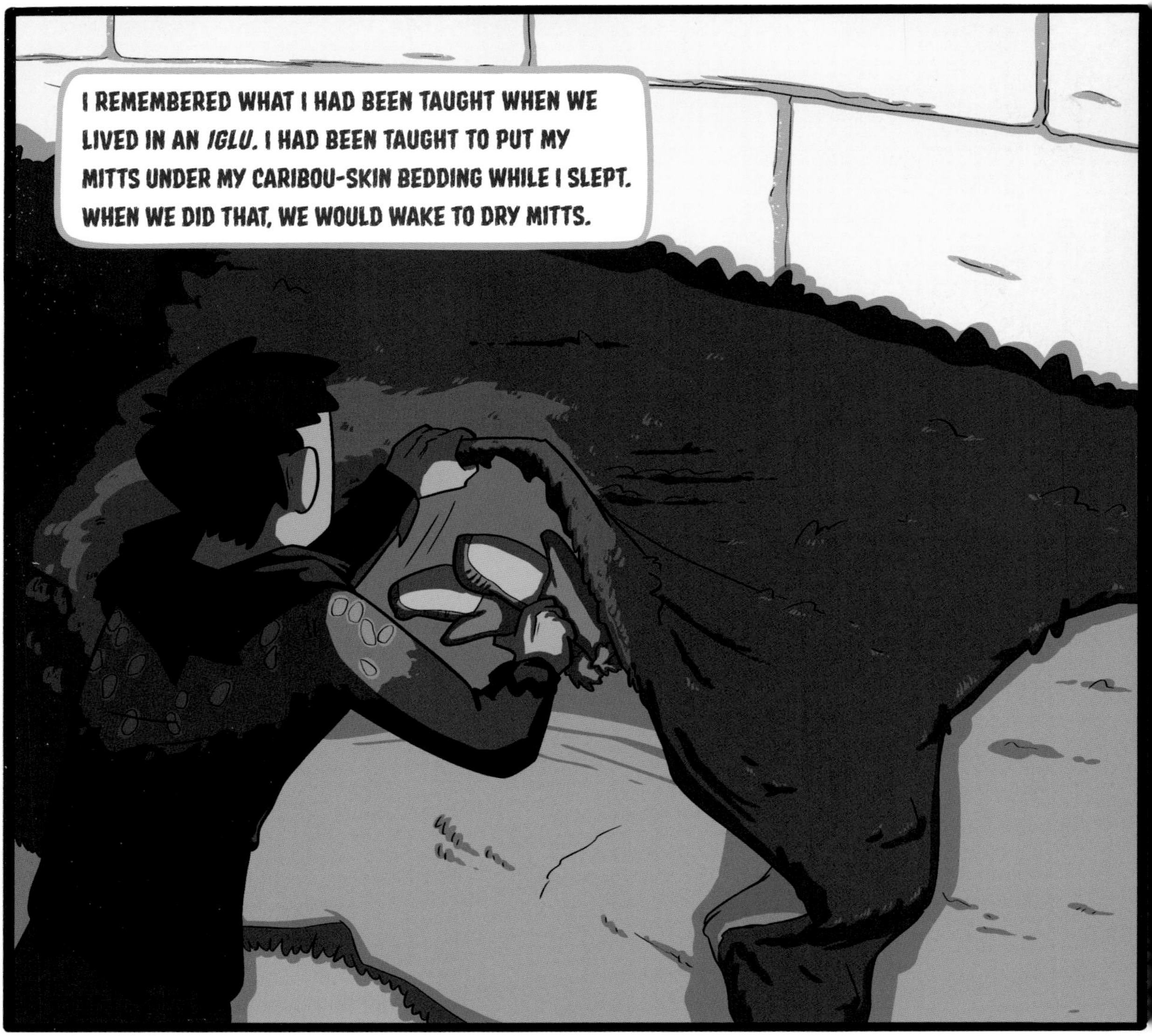
I REMEMBERED WHAT I HAD BEEN TAUGHT WHEN WE LIVED IN AN *IGLU*. I HAD BEEN TAUGHT TO PUT MY MITTS UNDER MY CARIBOU-SKIN BEDDING WHILE I SLEPT. WHEN WE DID THAT, WE WOULD WAKE TO DRY MITTS.

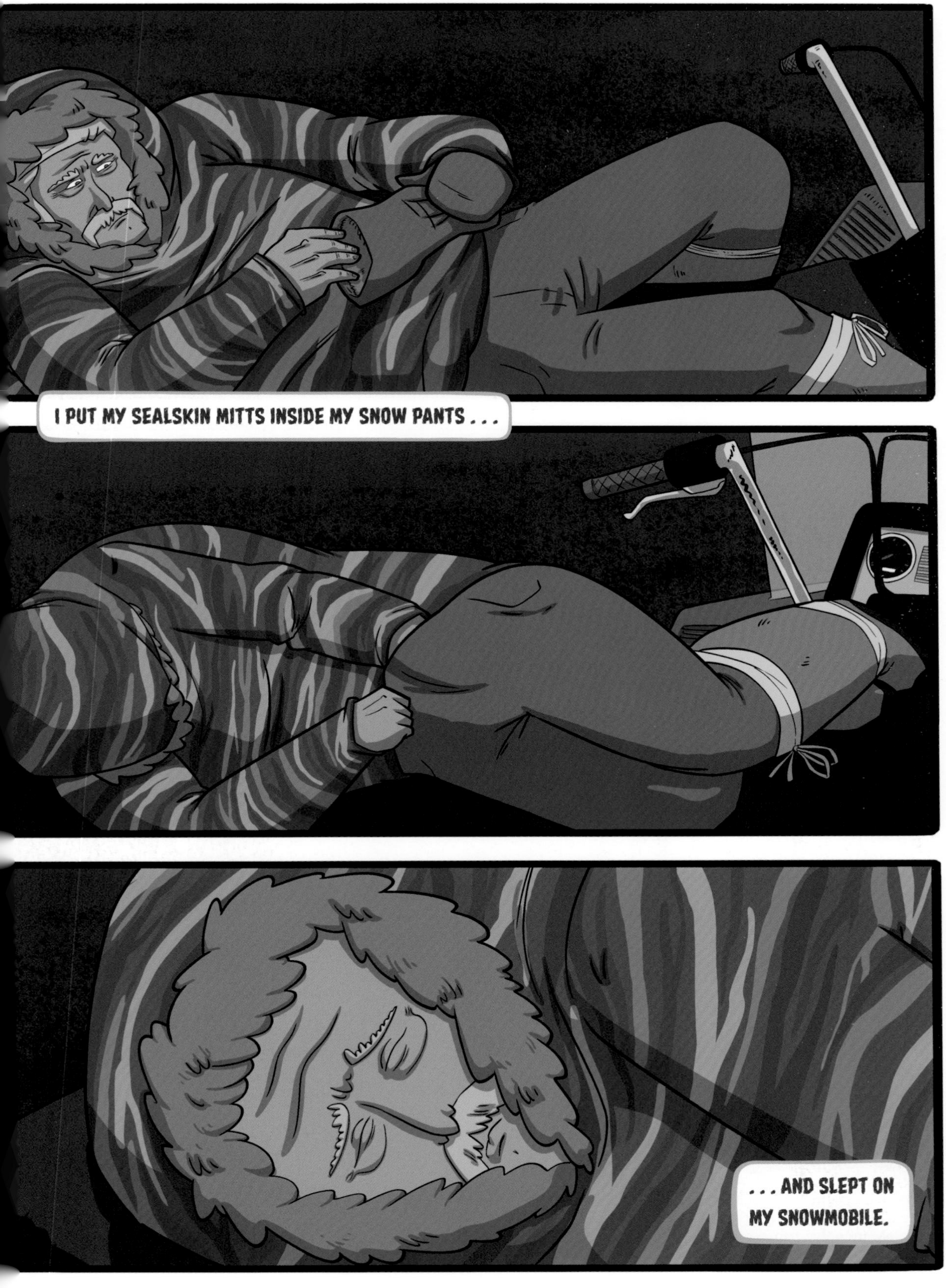
I PUT MY SEALSKIN MITTS INSIDE MY SNOW PANTS . . .
. . . AND SLEPT ON MY SNOWMOBILE.

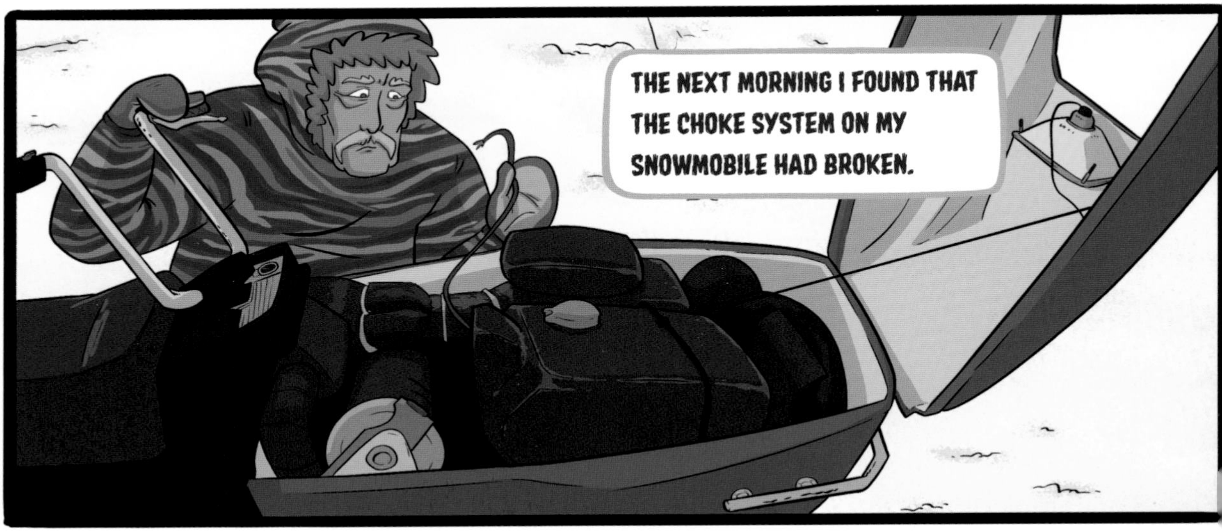
THE NEXT MORNING I FOUND THAT THE CHOKE SYSTEM ON MY SNOWMOBILE HAD BROKEN.

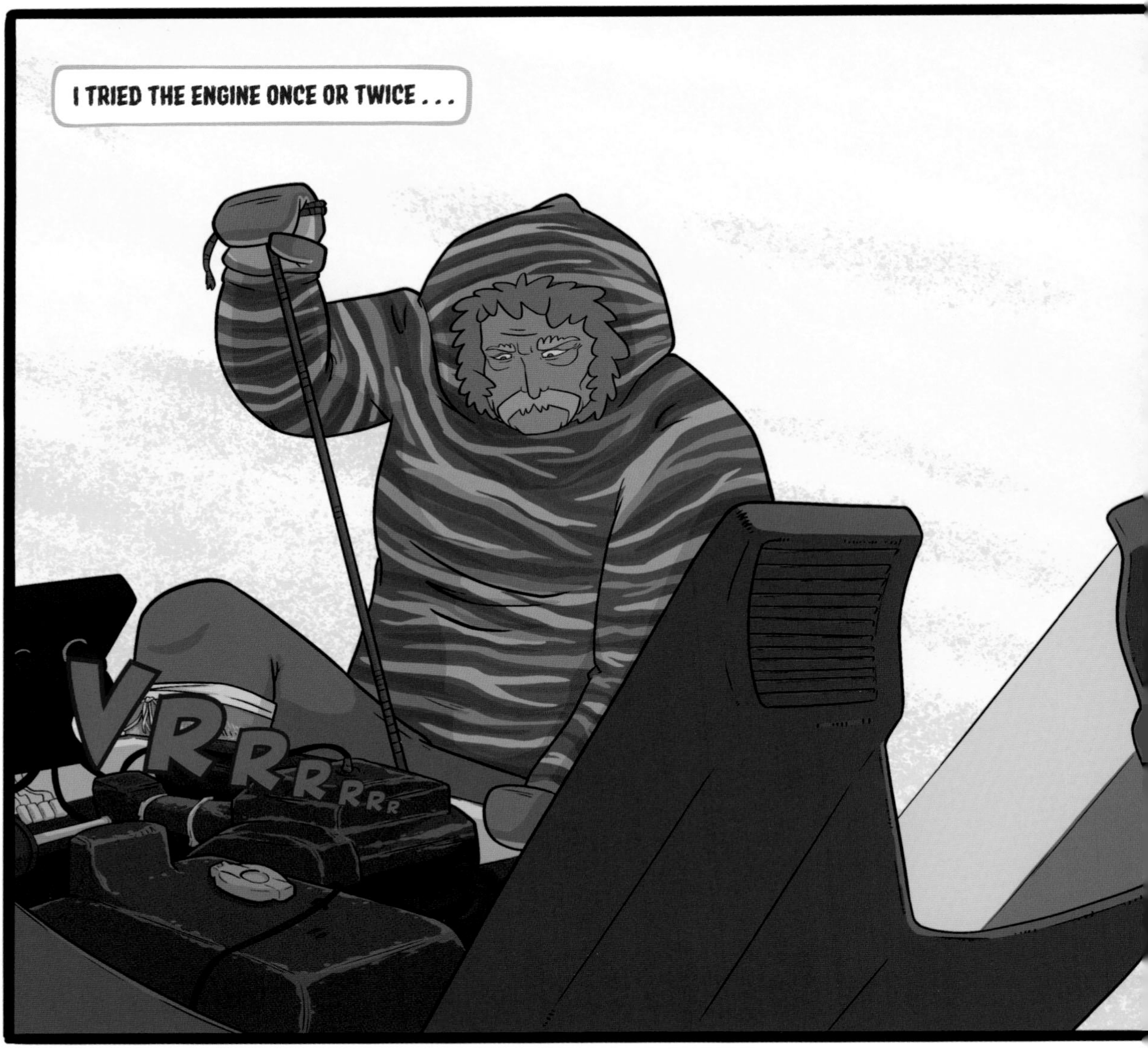
I TRIED THE ENGINE ONCE OR TWICE . . .
VRRRRRR

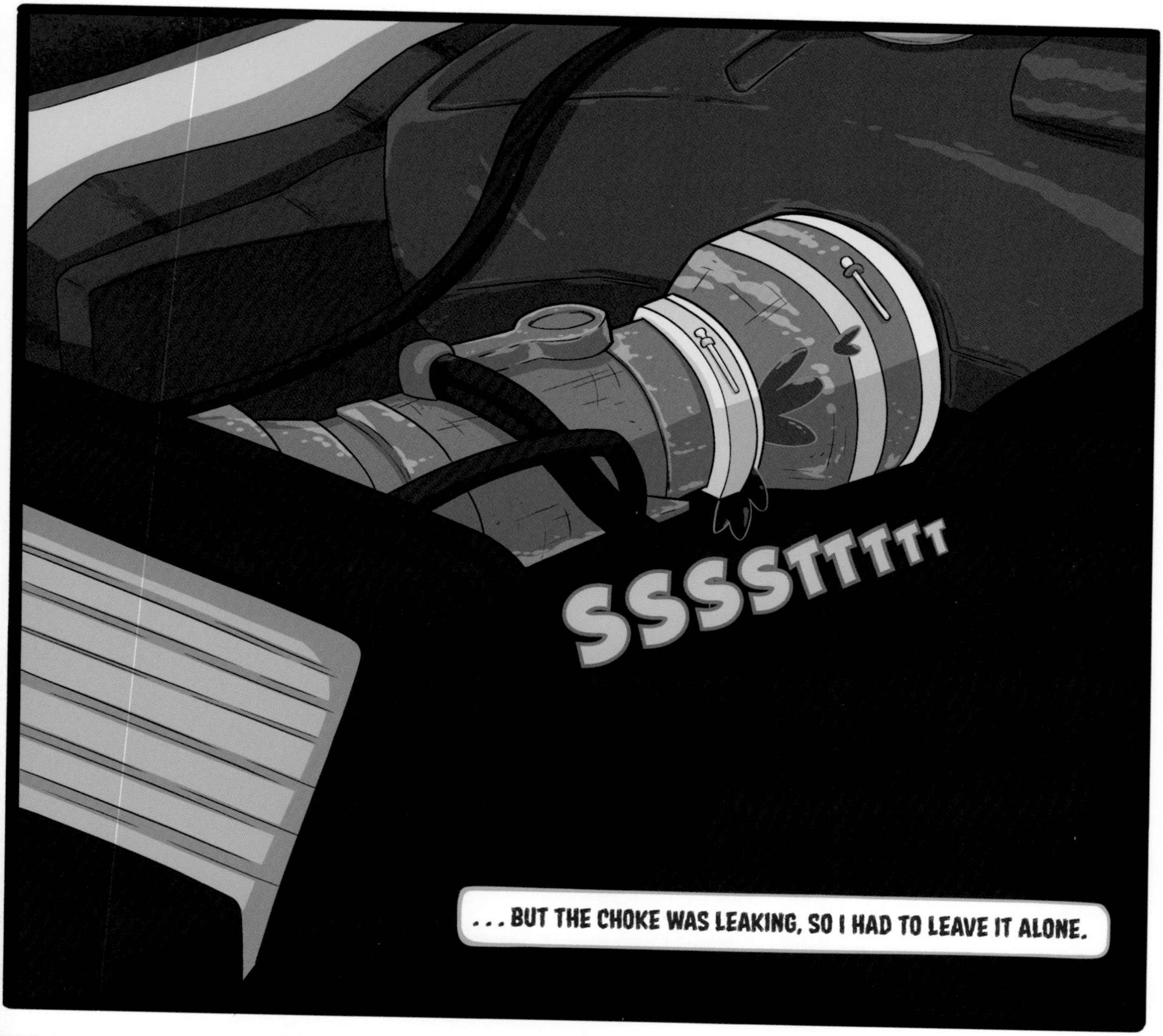
SSSSTTTTT
. . . BUT THE CHOKE WAS LEAKING, SO I HAD TO LEAVE IT ALONE.

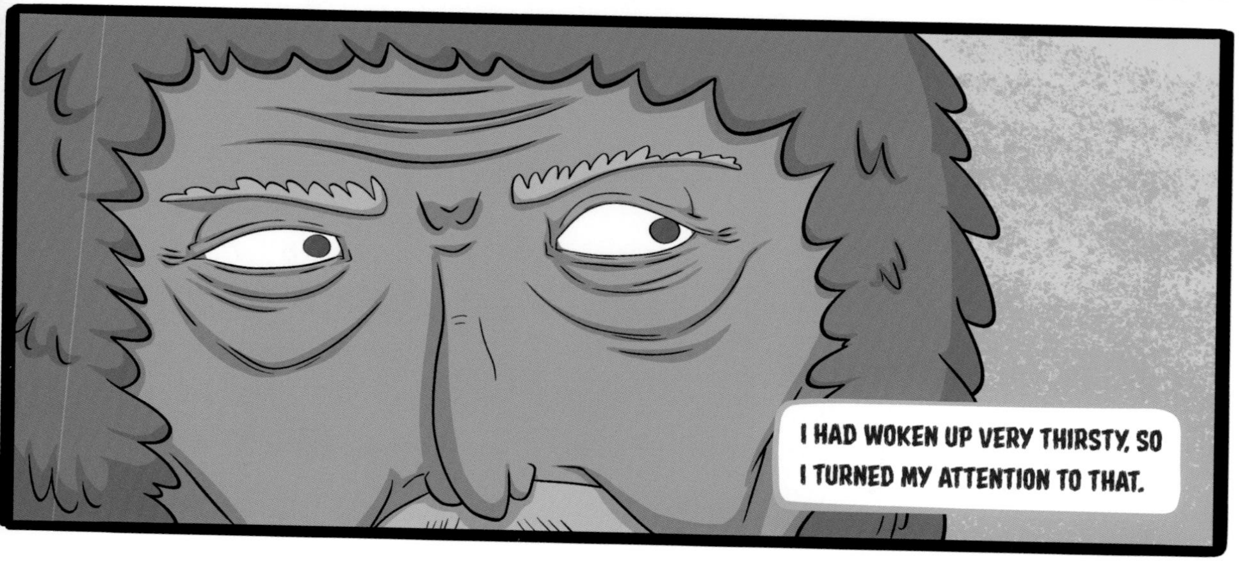
I HAD WOKEN UP VERY THIRSTY, SO I TURNED MY ATTENTION TO THAT.

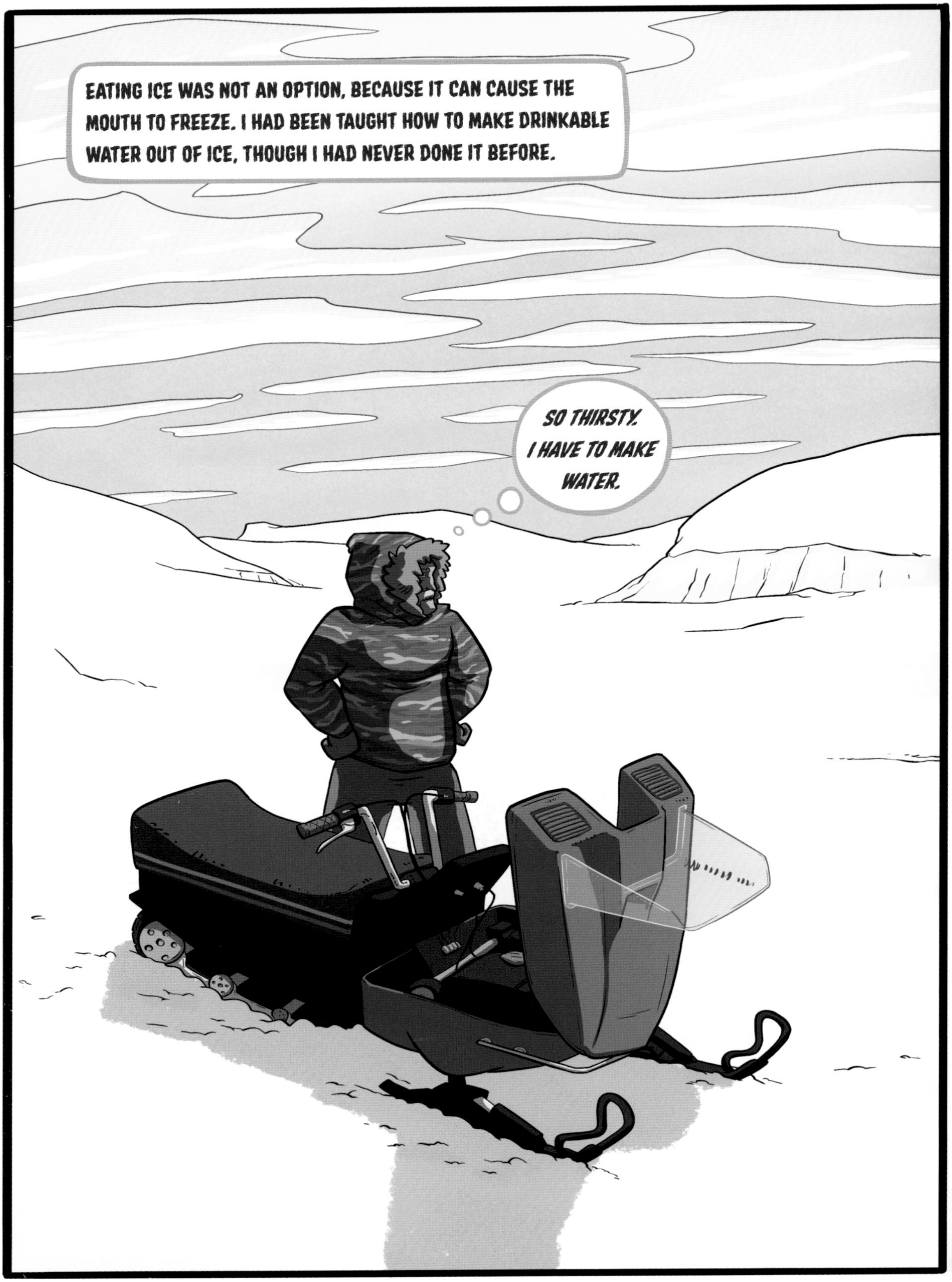
EATING ICE WAS NOT AN OPTION, BECAUSE IT CAN CAUSE THE MOUTH TO FREEZE. I HAD BEEN TAUGHT HOW TO MAKE DRINKABLE WATER OUT OF ICE, THOUGH I HAD NEVER DONE IT BEFORE.
SO THIRSTY. I HAVE TO MAKE WATER.

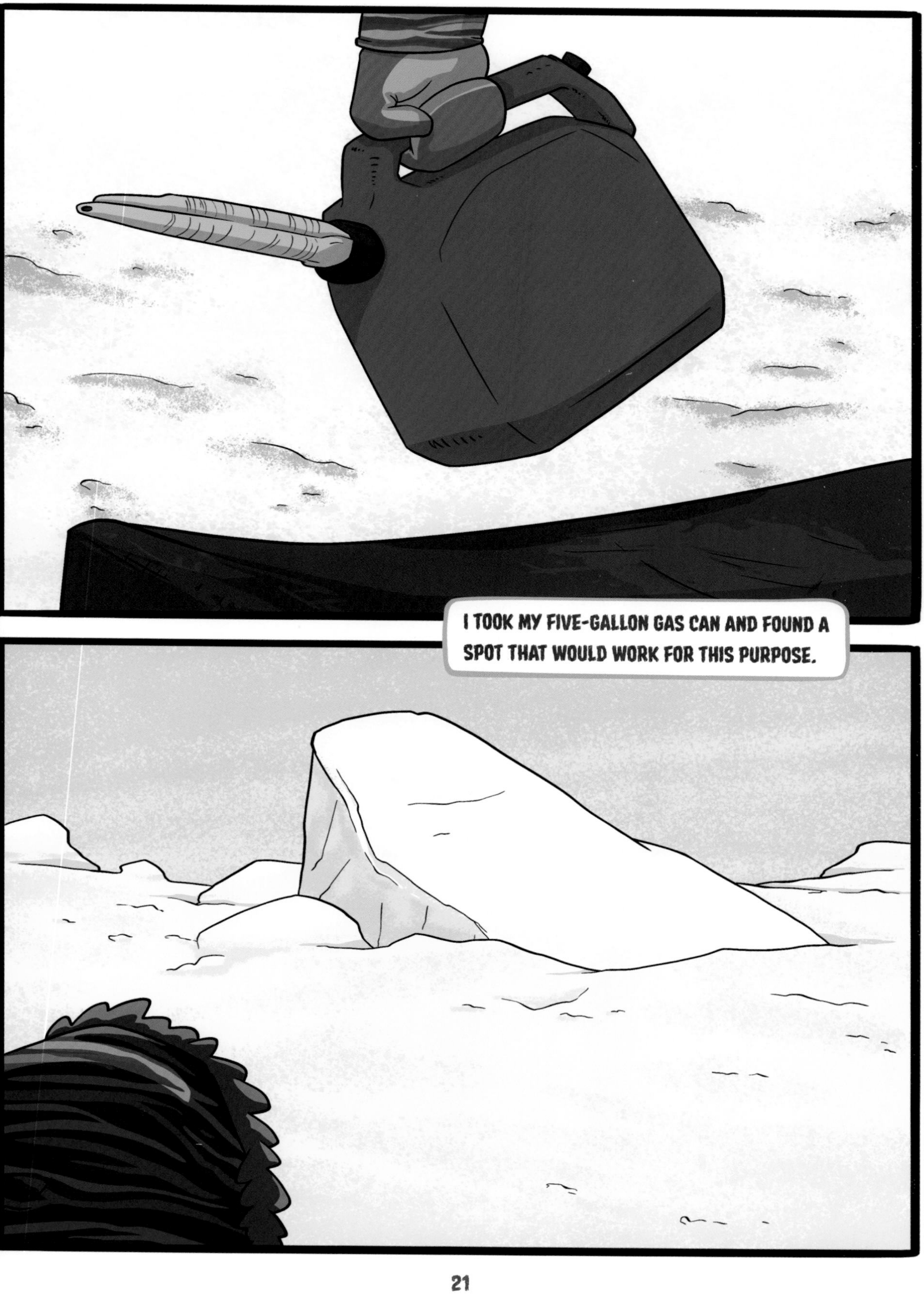
I TOOK MY FIVE-GALLON GAS CAN AND FOUND A SPOT THAT WOULD WORK FOR THIS PURPOSE.

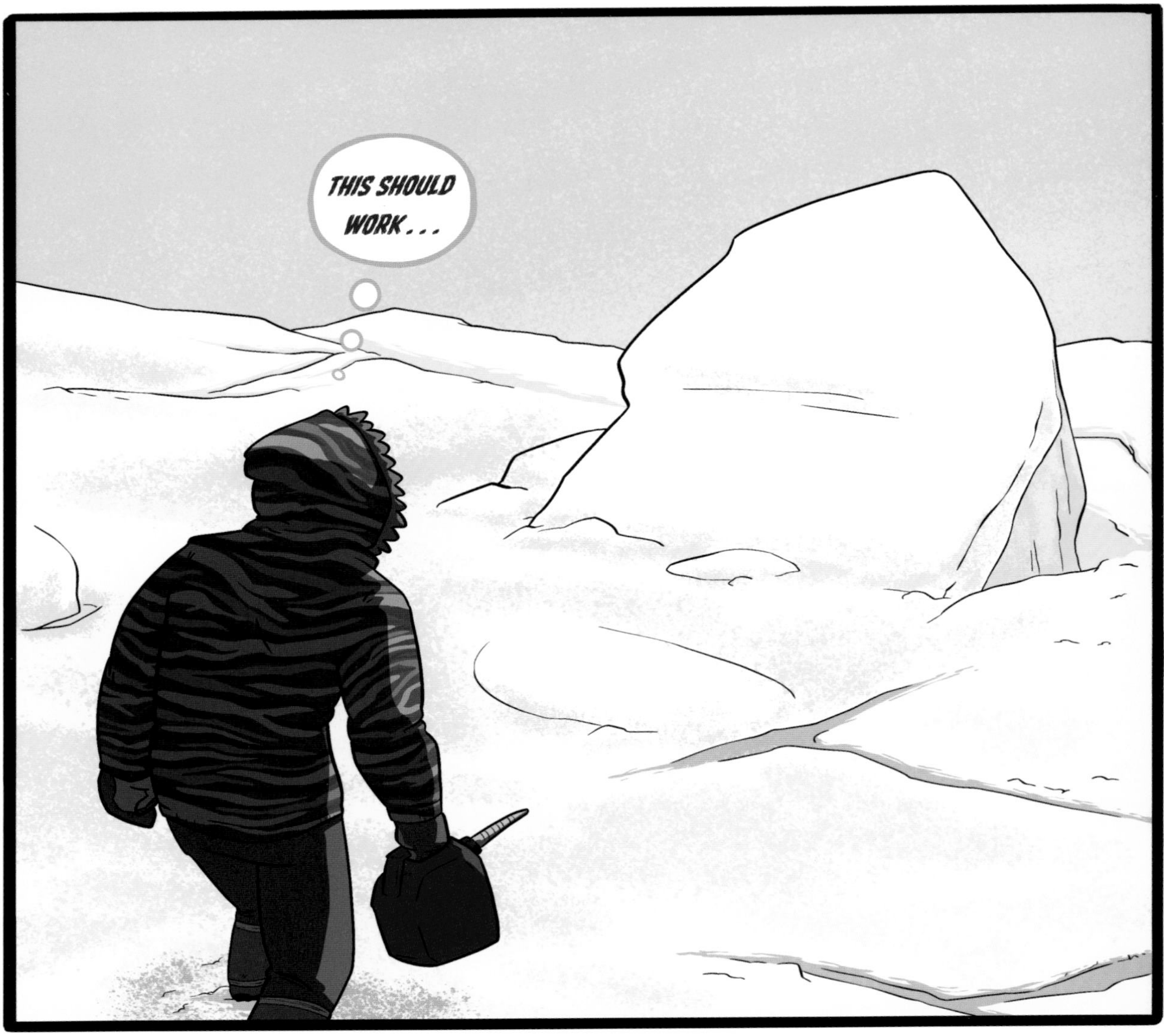
THIS SHOULD WORK . . .

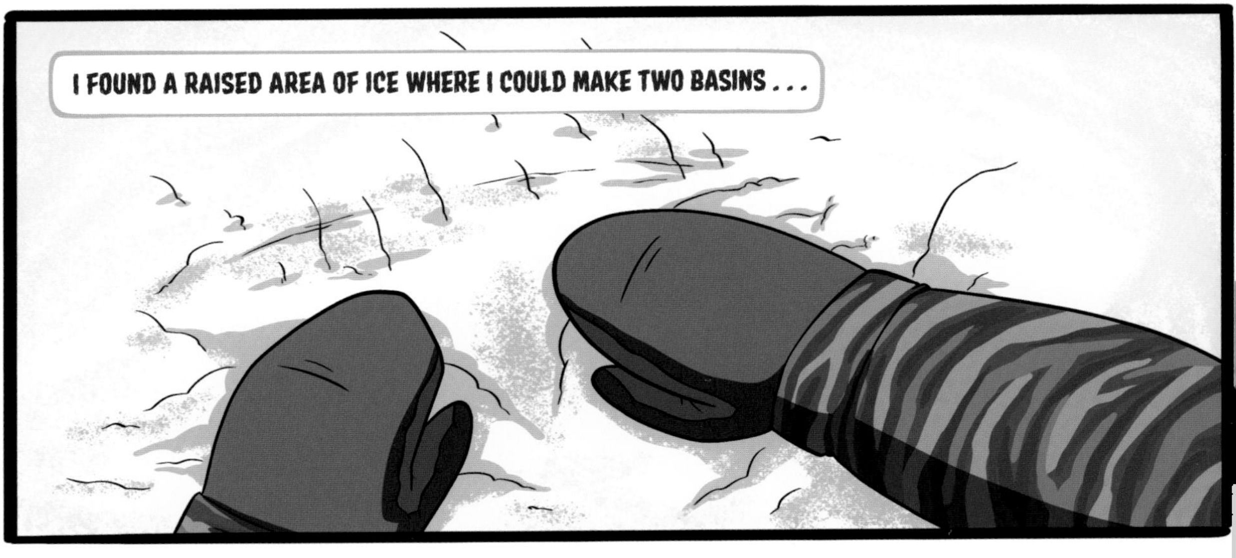
I FOUND A RAISED AREA OF ICE WHERE I COULD MAKE TWO BASINS . . .

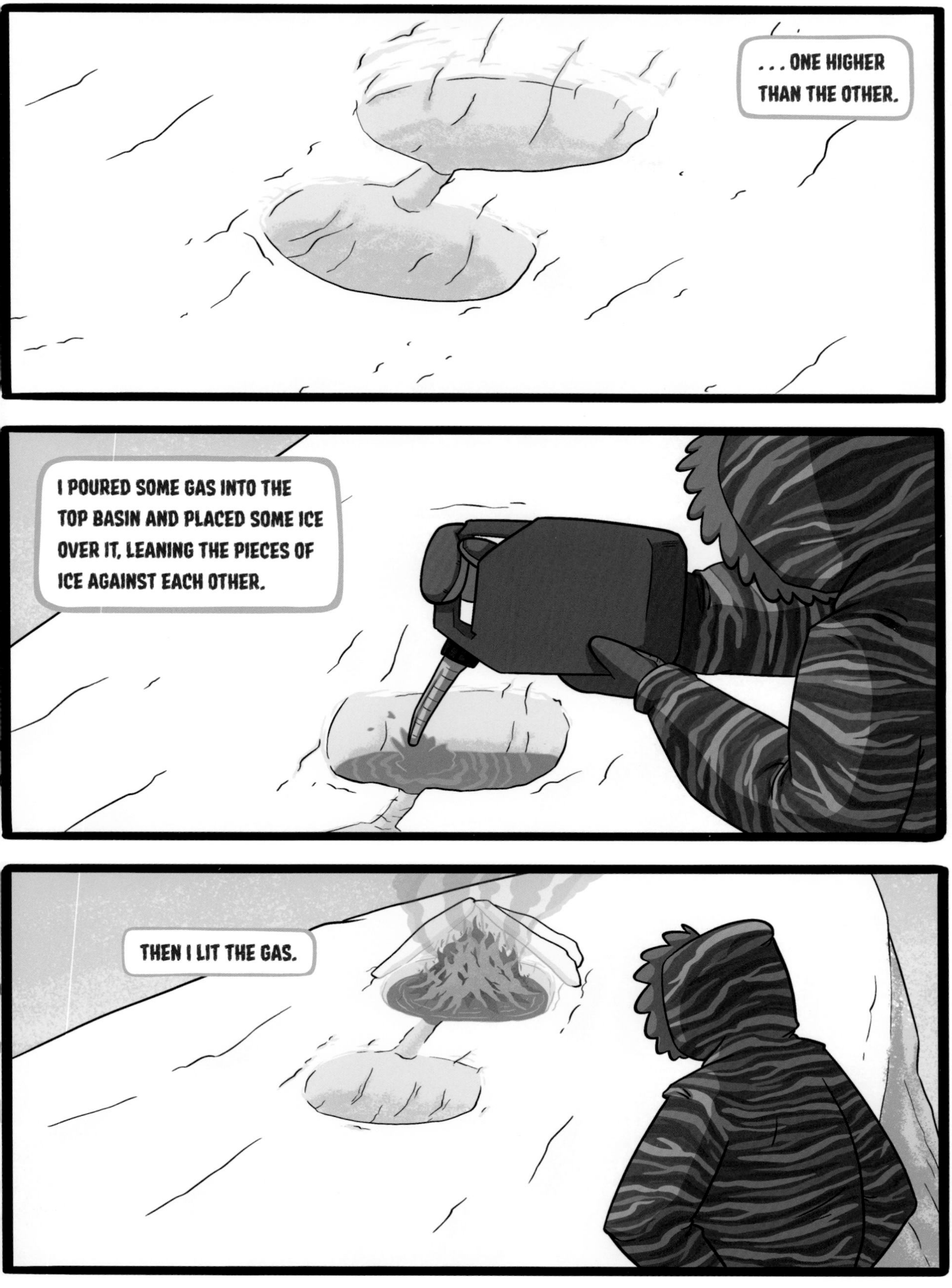
. . . ONE HIGHER THAN THE OTHER.
I POURED SOME GAS INTO THE TOP BASIN AND PLACED SOME ICE OVER IT, LEANING THE PIECES OF ICE AGAINST EACH OTHER.
THEN I LIT THE GAS.

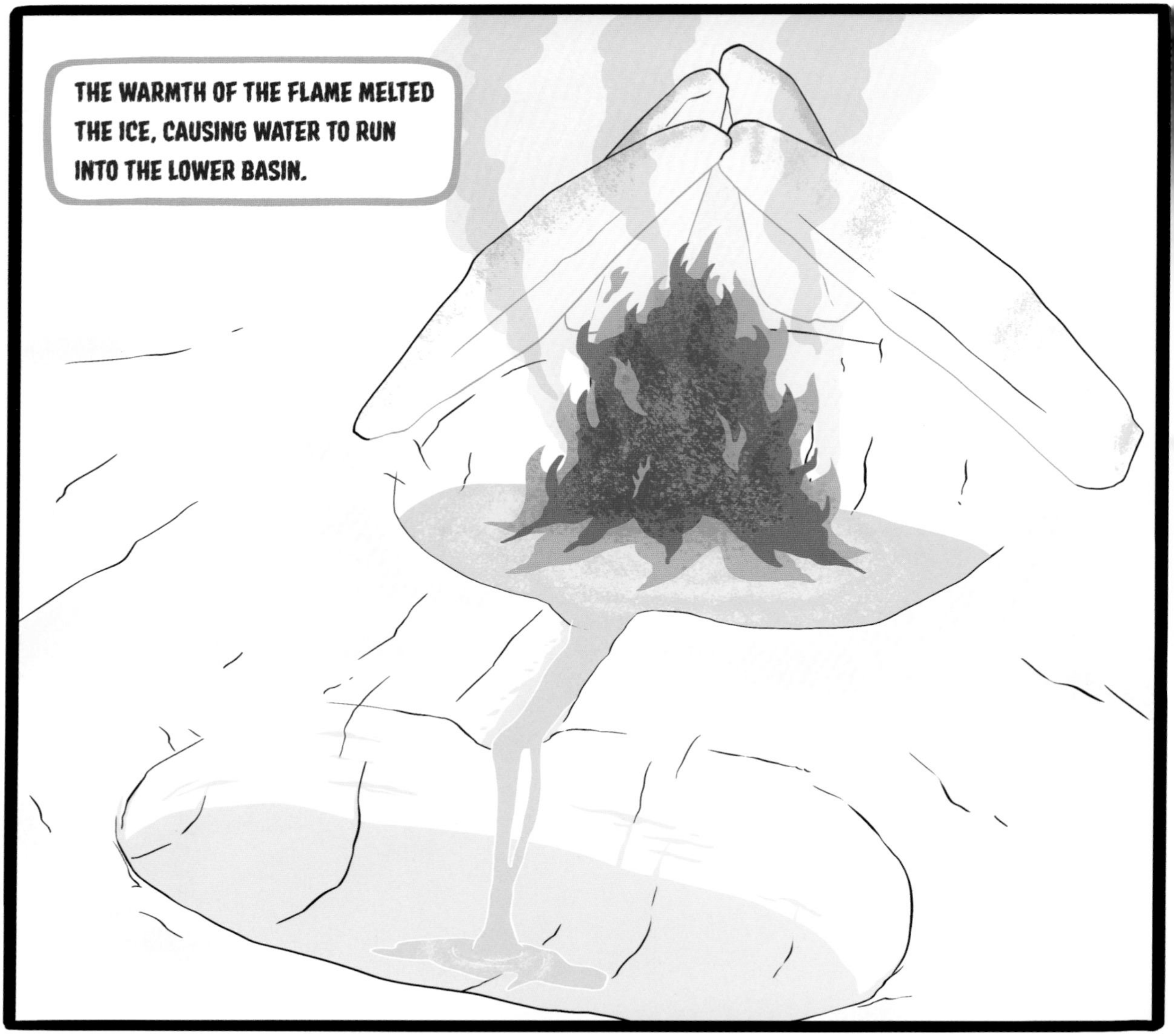
THE WARMTH OF THE FLAME MELTED THE ICE, CAUSING WATER TO RUN INTO THE LOWER BASIN.

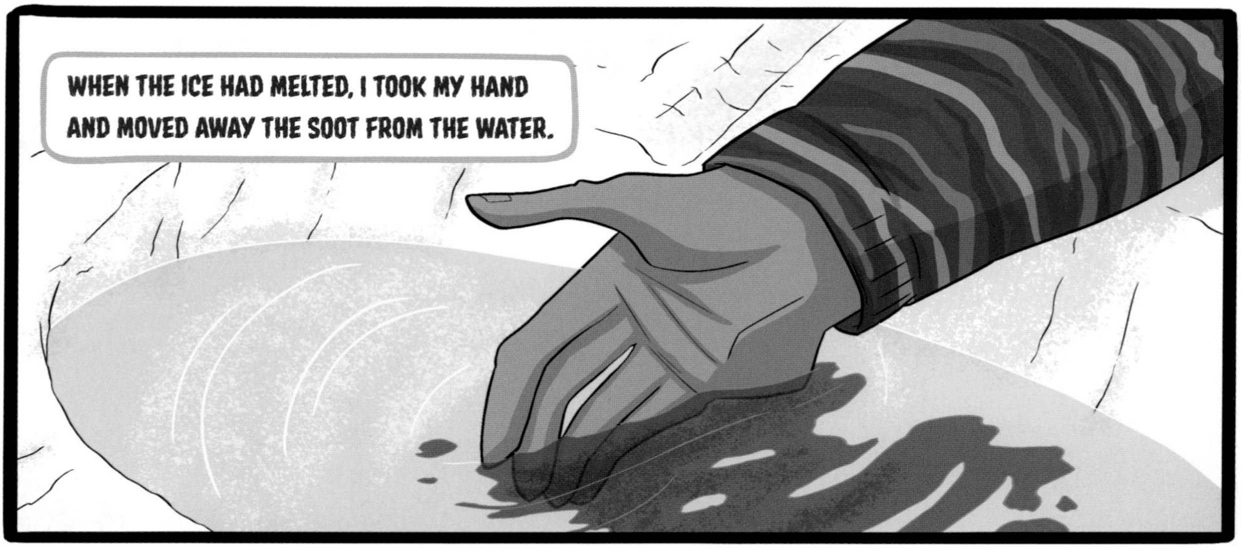
WHEN THE ICE HAD MELTED, I TOOK MY HAND AND MOVED AWAY THE SOOT FROM THE WATER.

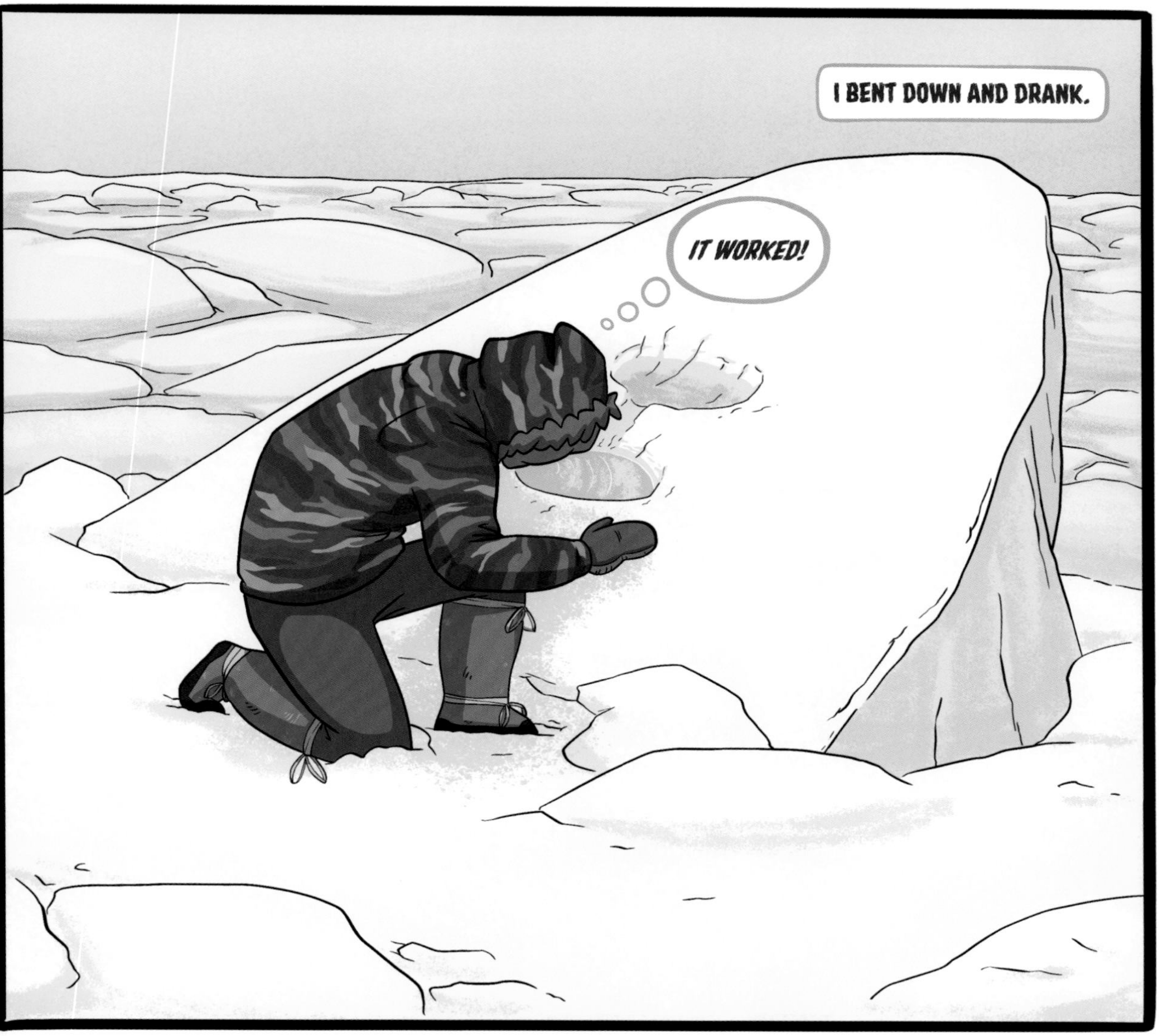
I BENT DOWN AND DRANK.
IT WORKED!

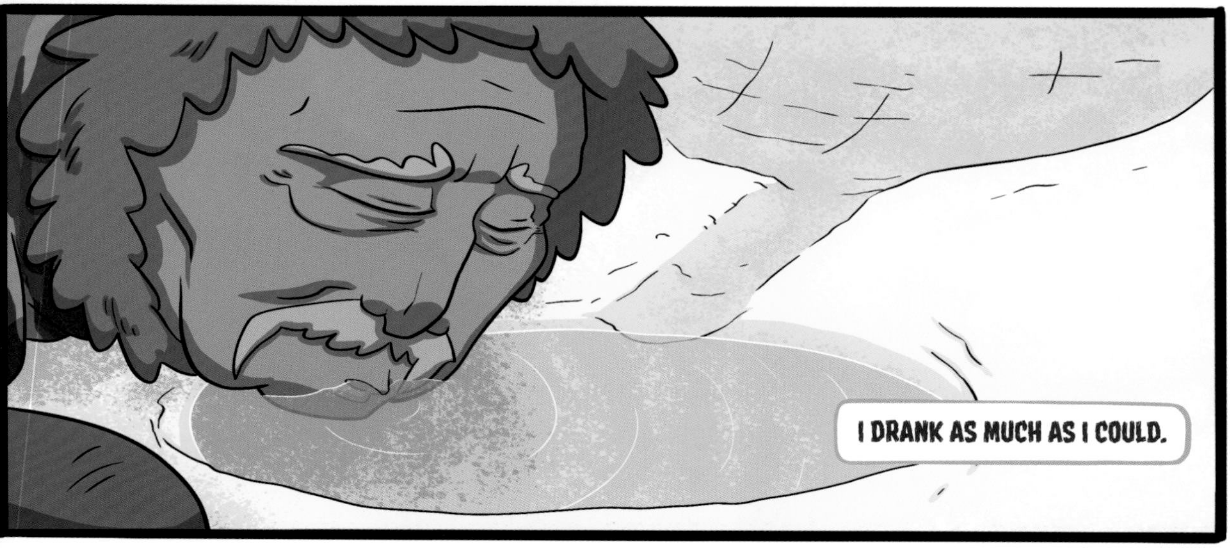
I DRANK AS MUCH AS I COULD.

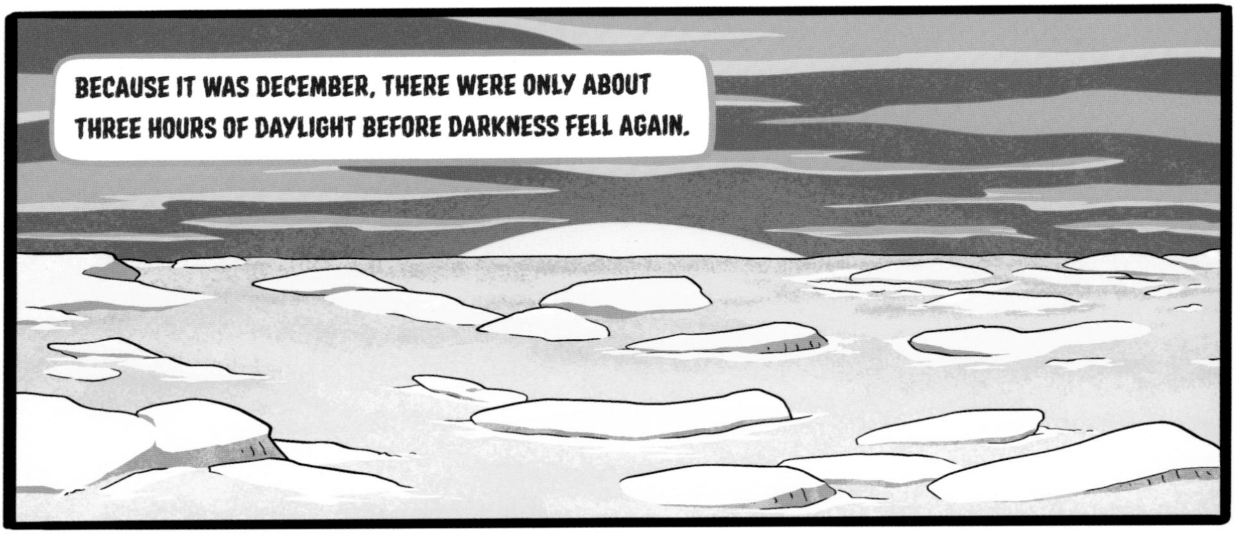
BECAUSE IT WAS DECEMBER, THERE WERE ONLY ABOUT THREE HOURS OF DAYLIGHT BEFORE DARKNESS FELL AGAIN.

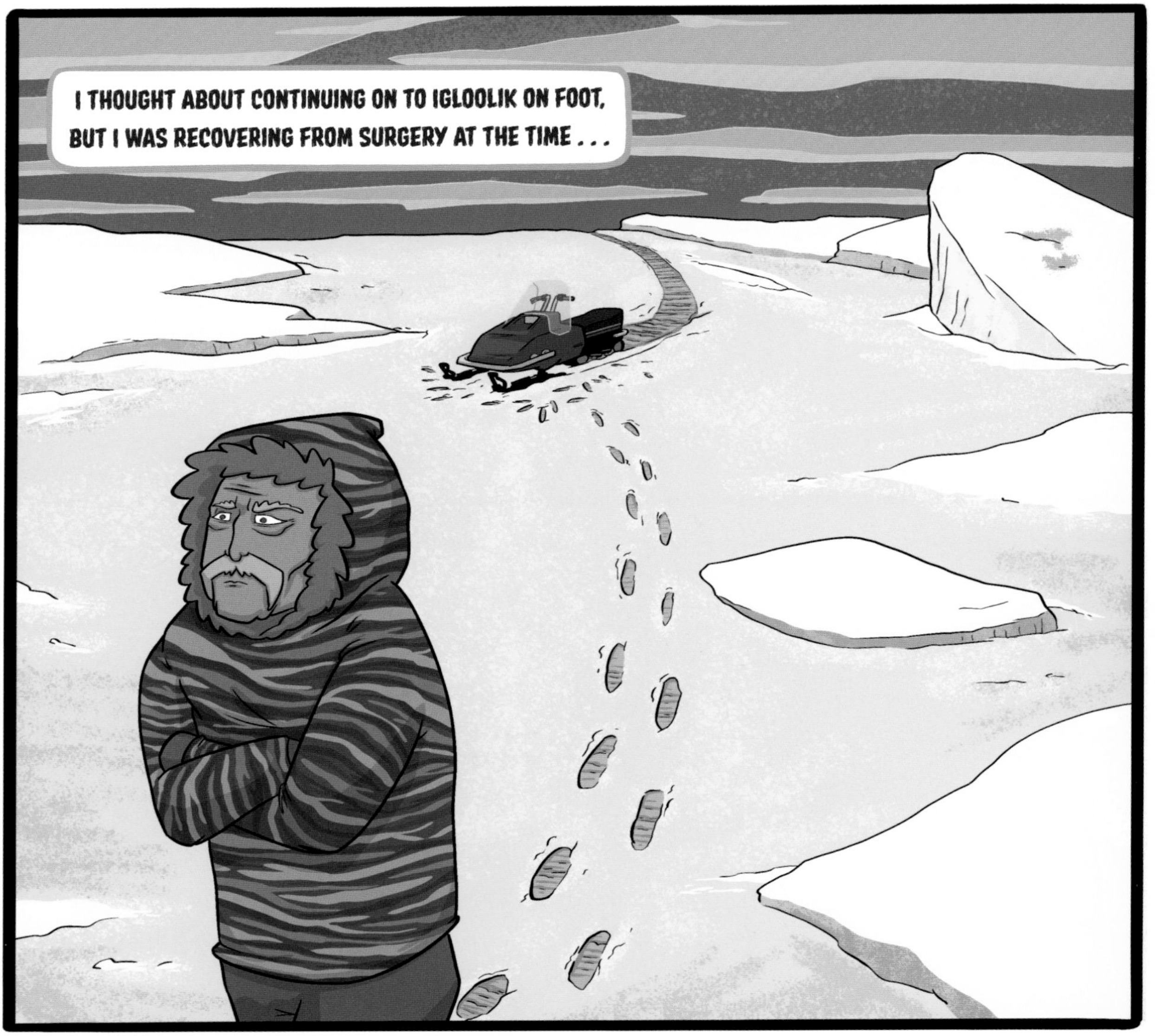
I THOUGHT ABOUT CONTINUING ON TO IGLOOLIK ON FOOT, BUT I WAS RECOVERING FROM SURGERY AT THE TIME . . .

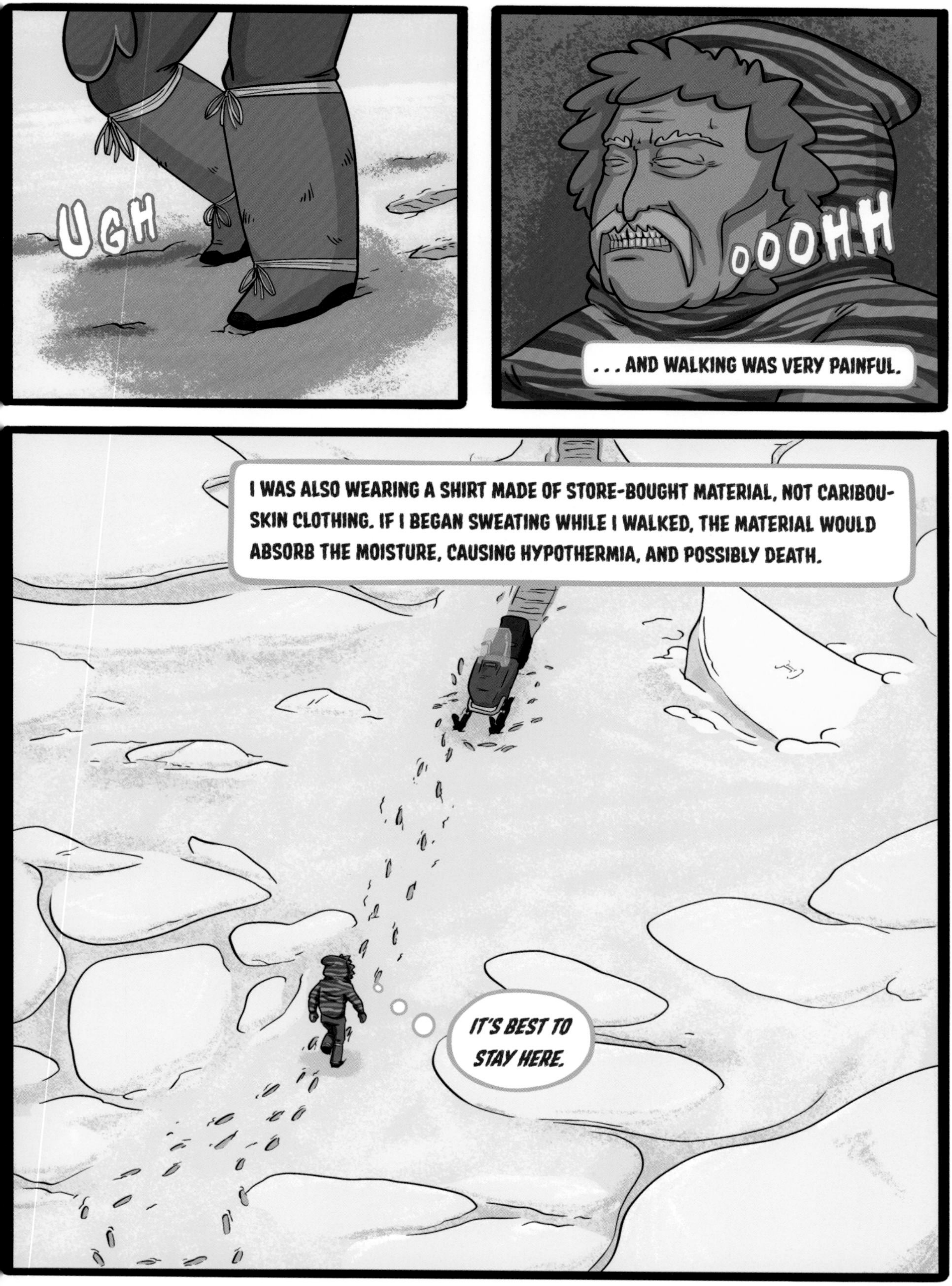
UGH
OOOHH
. . . AND WALKING WAS VERY PAINFUL.
I WAS ALSO WEARING A SHIRT MADE OF STORE-BOUGHT MATERIAL, NOT CARIBOU-SKIN CLOTHING. IF I BEGAN SWEATING WHILE I WALKED, THE MATERIAL WOULD ABSORB THE MOISTURE, CAUSING HYPOTHERMIA, AND POSSIBLY DEATH.
IT'S BEST TO STAY HERE.

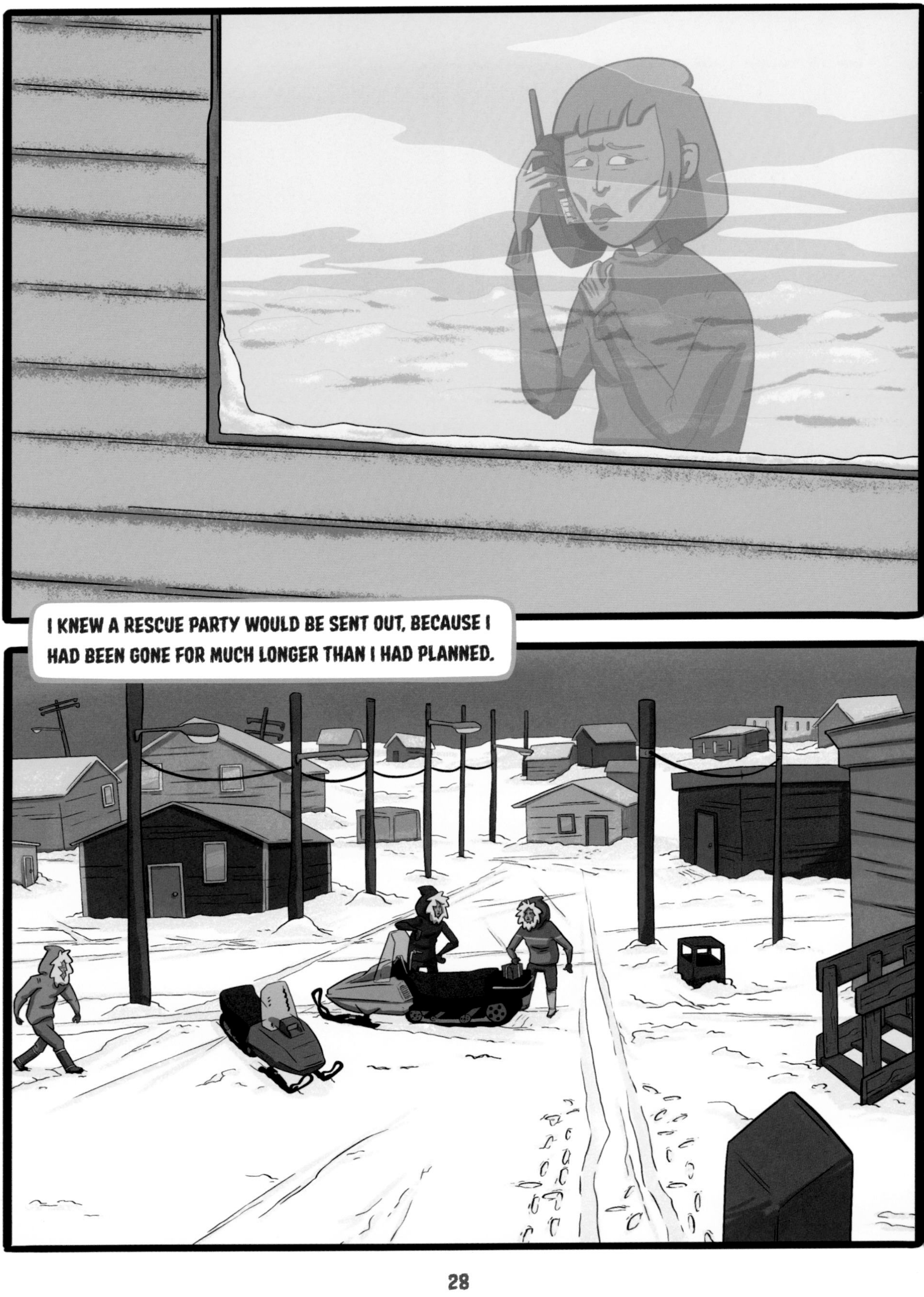
I KNEW A RESCUE PARTY WOULD BE SENT OUT, BECAUSE I HAD BEEN GONE FOR MUCH LONGER THAN I HAD PLANNED.

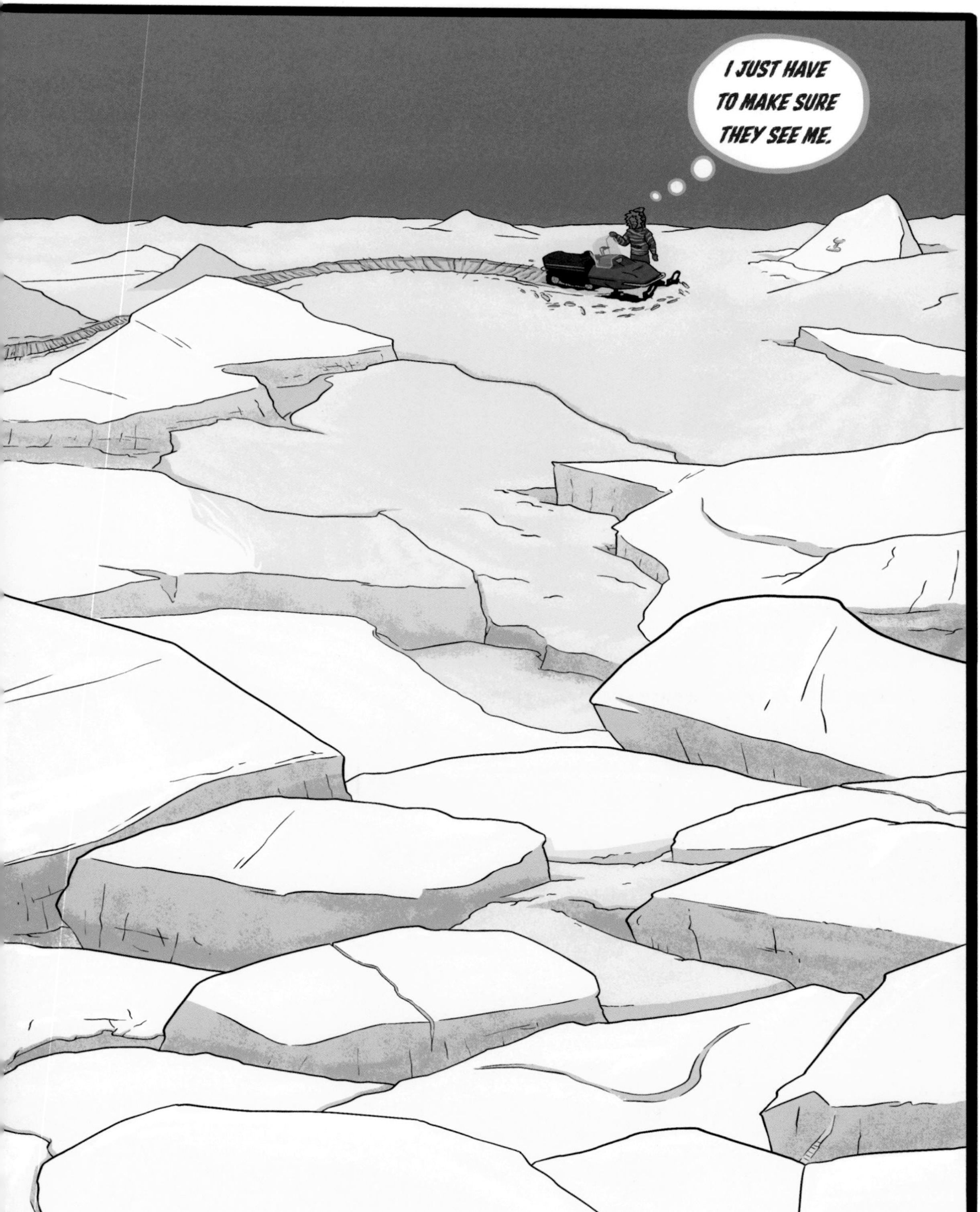
I JUST HAVE
TO MAKE SURE
THEY SEE ME.

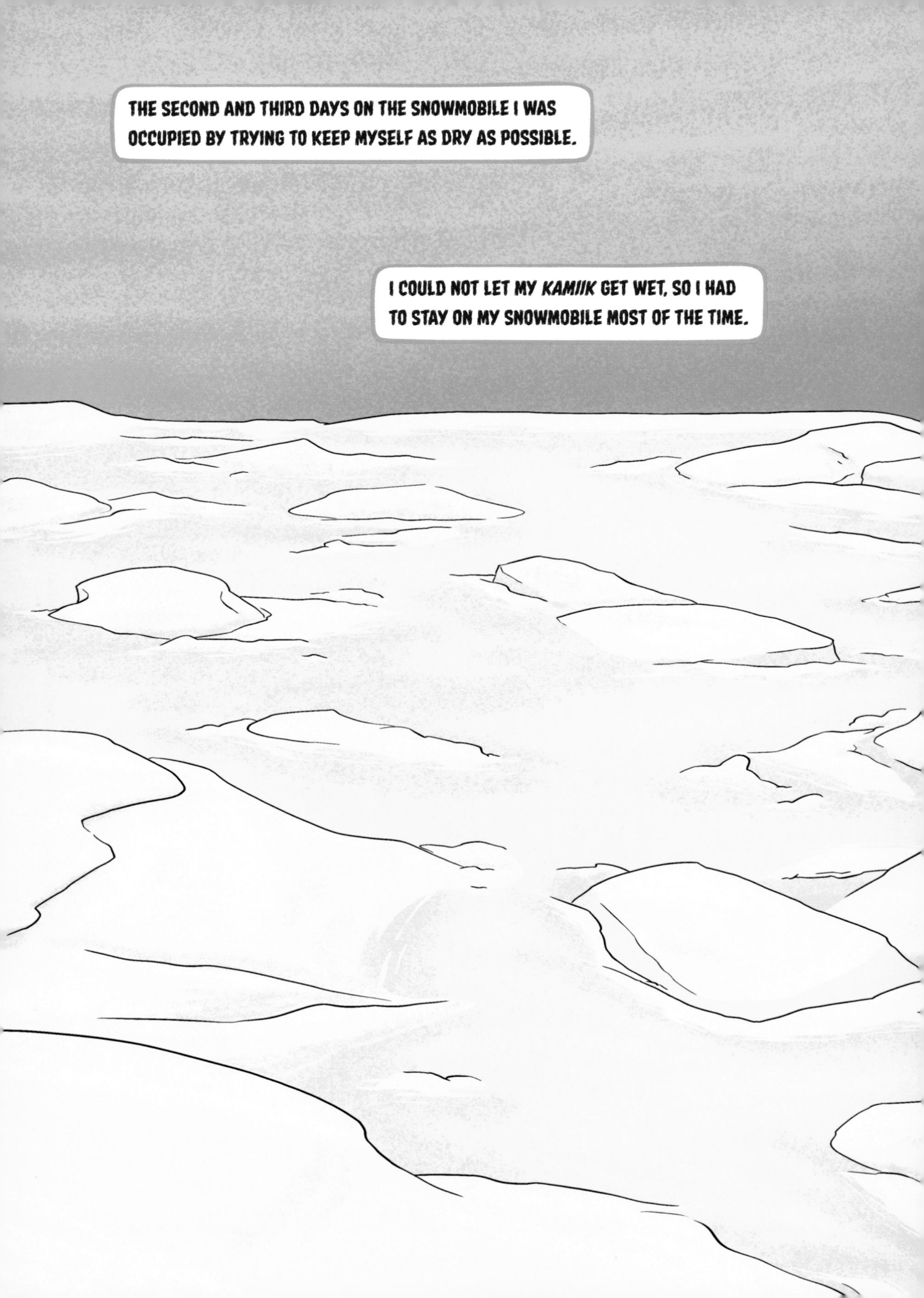
THE SECOND AND THIRD DAYS ON THE SNOWMOBILE I WAS OCCUPIED BY TRYING TO KEEP MYSELF AS DRY AS POSSIBLE.
I COULD NOT LET MY *KAMIIK* GET WET, SO I HAD TO STAY ON MY SNOWMOBILE MOST OF THE TIME.

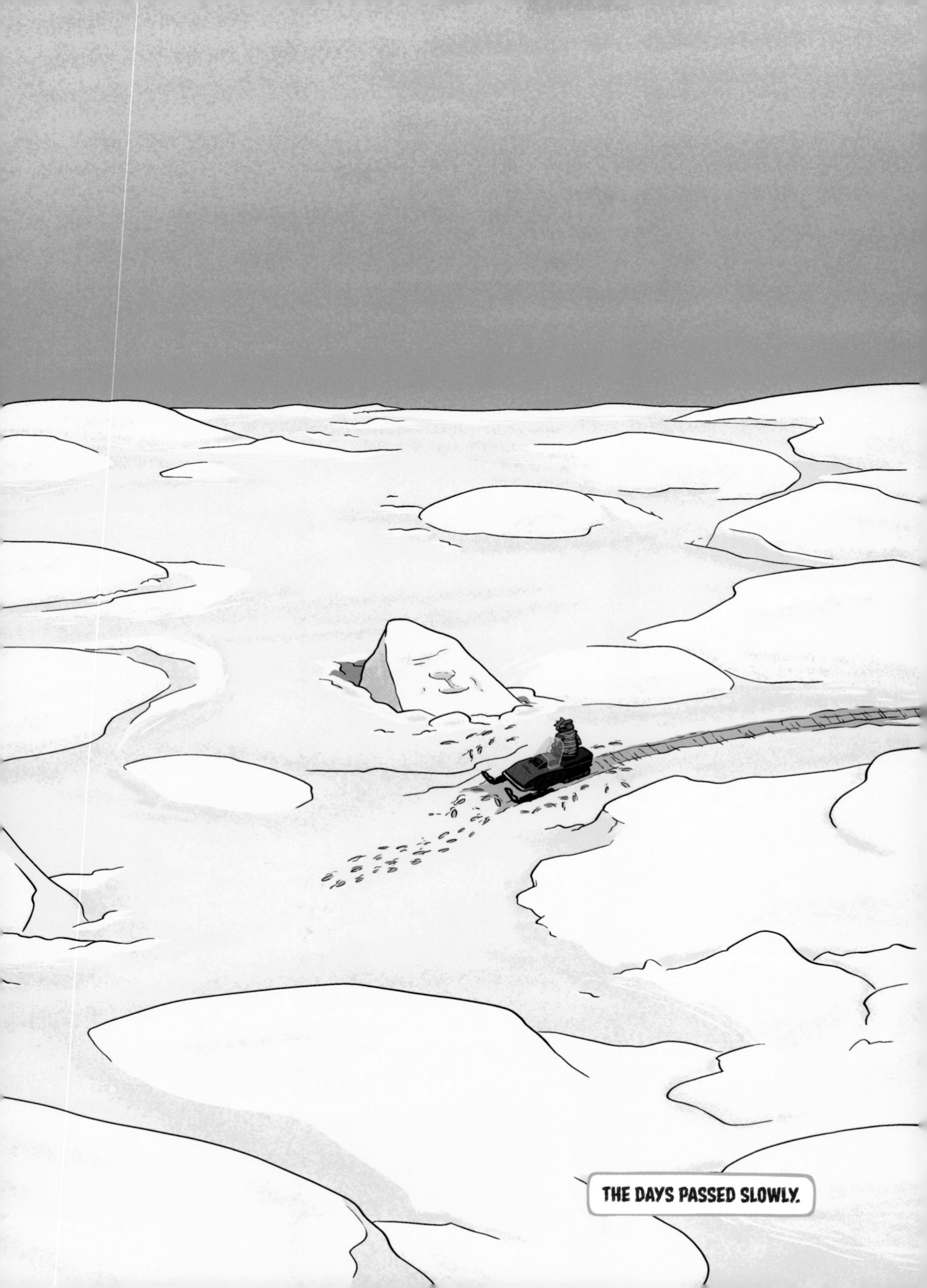
THE DAYS PASSED SLOWLY.

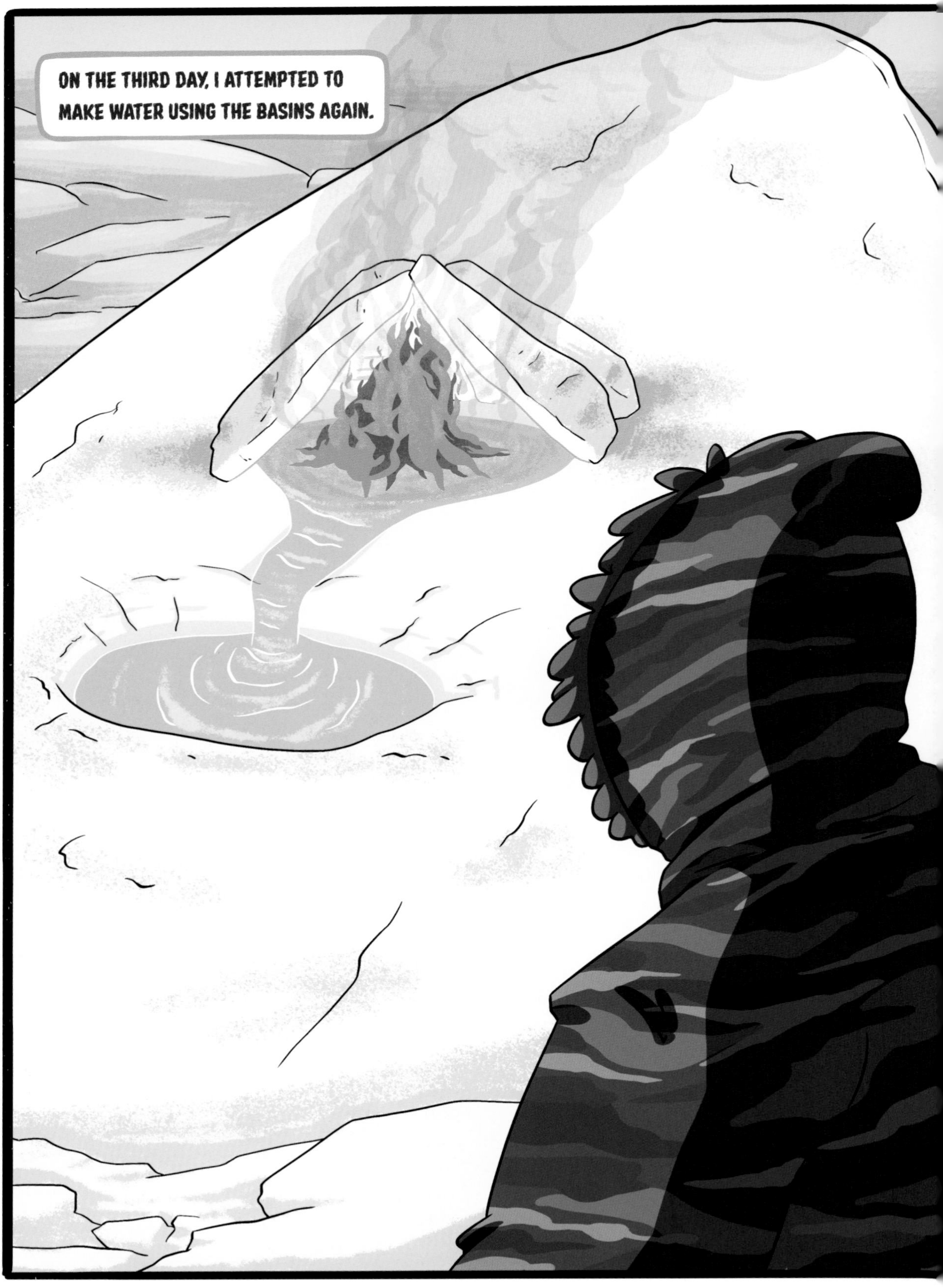
ON THE THIRD DAY, I ATTEMPTED TO MAKE WATER USING THE BASINS AGAIN.

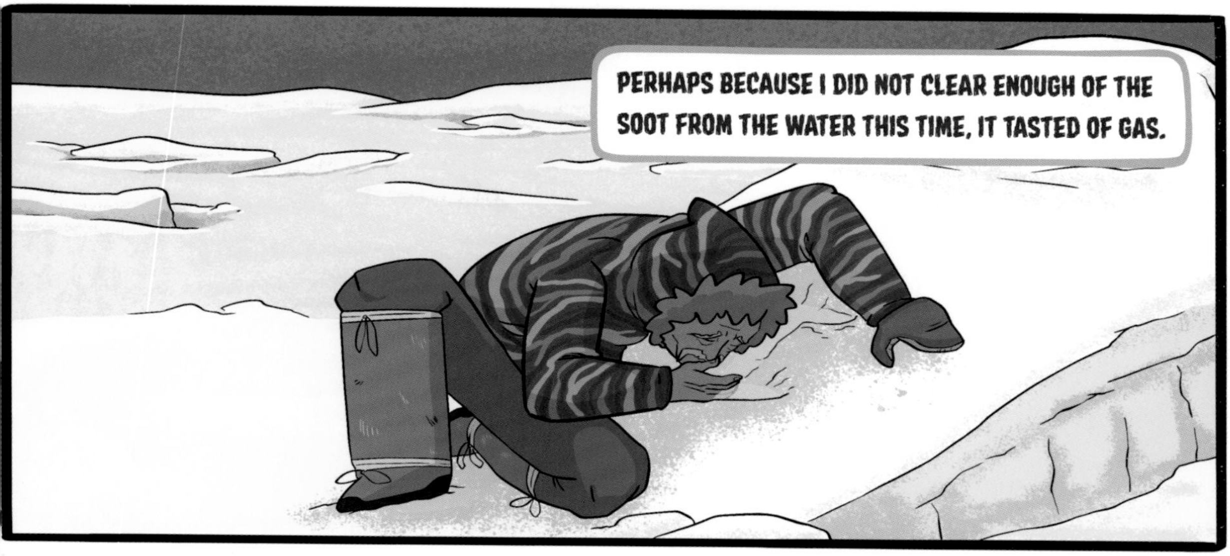
PERHAPS BECAUSE I DID NOT CLEAR ENOUGH OF THE SOOT FROM THE WATER THIS TIME, IT TASTED OF GAS.

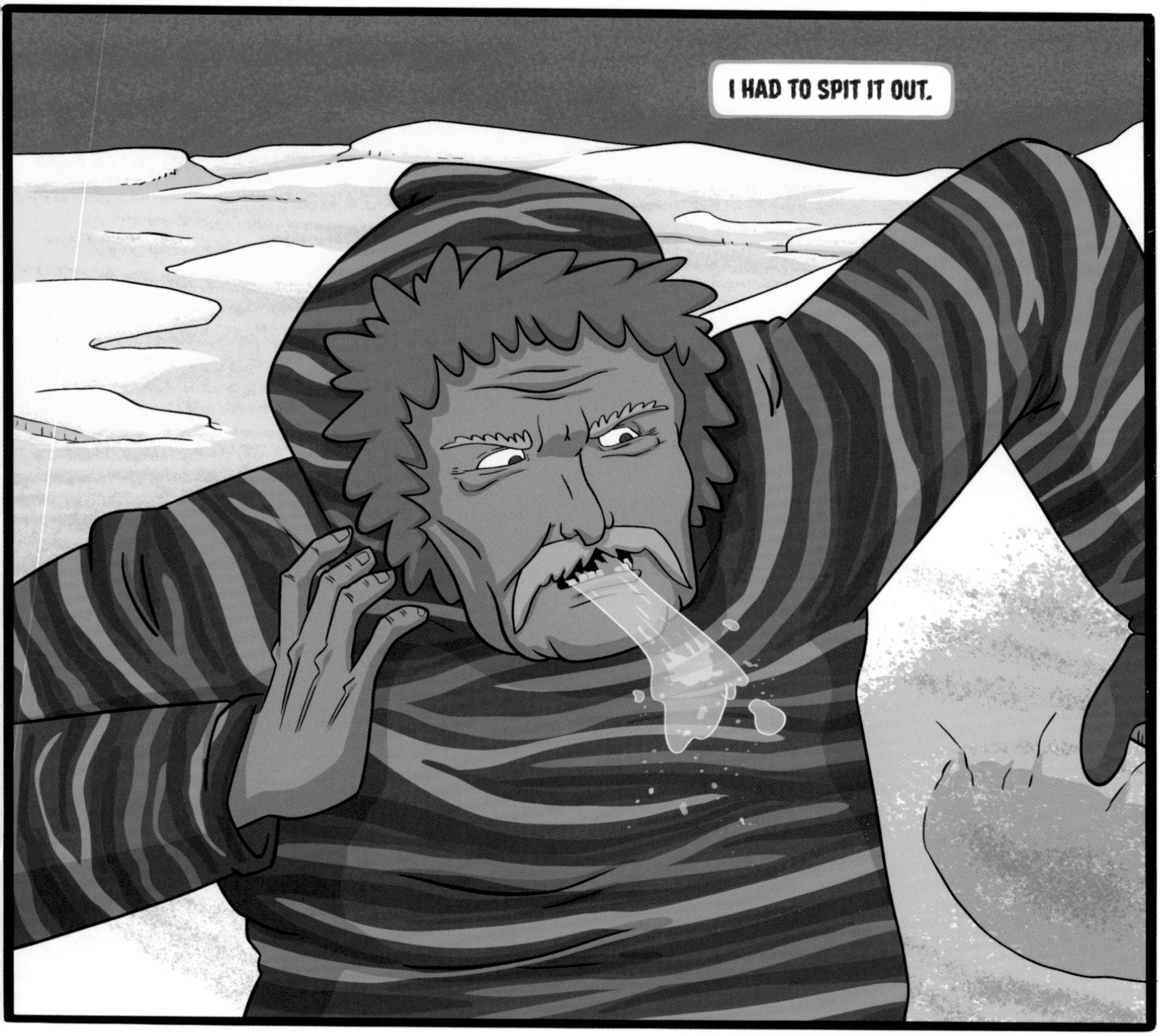
I HAD TO SPIT IT OUT.

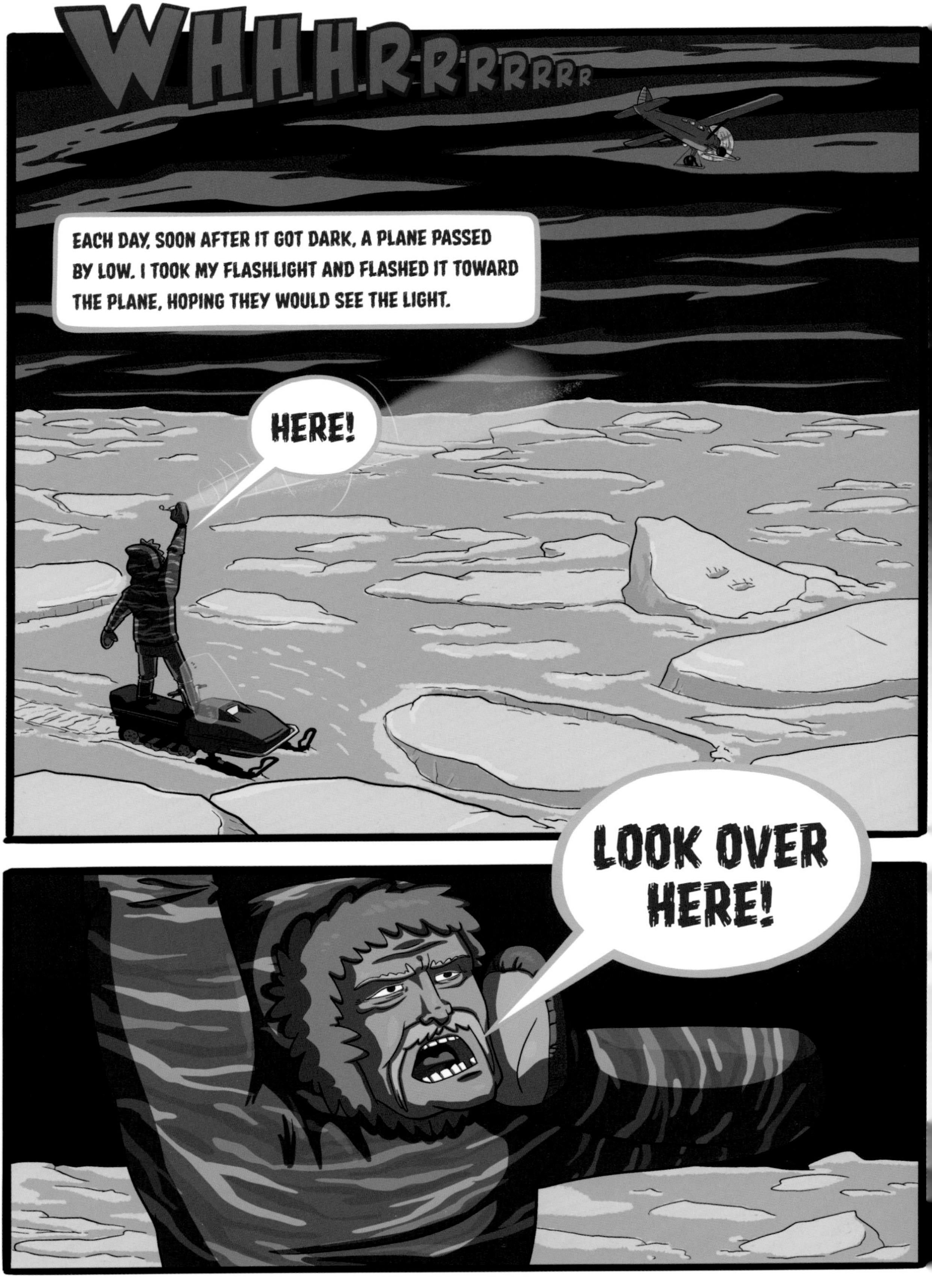
WHHHRRRRRRR
EACH DAY, SOON AFTER IT GOT DARK, A PLANE PASSED BY LOW. I TOOK MY FLASHLIGHT AND FLASHED IT TOWARD THE PLANE, HOPING THEY WOULD SEE THE LIGHT.
HERE!
LOOK OVER HERE!

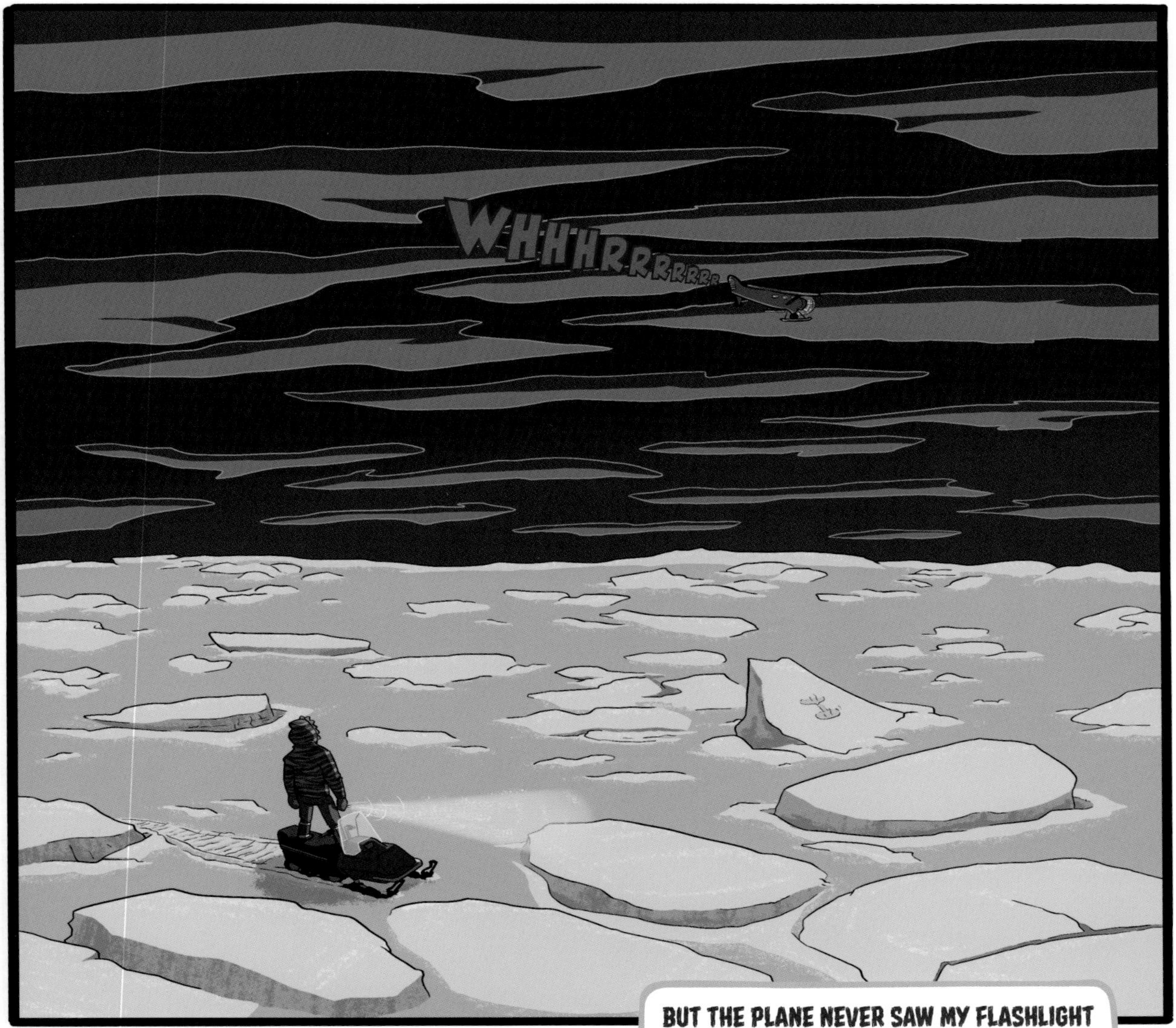
WHHHRRRRRRRR
BUT THE PLANE NEVER SAW MY FLASHLIGHT AND THEY WERE NOT ABLE TO SITUATE ME.

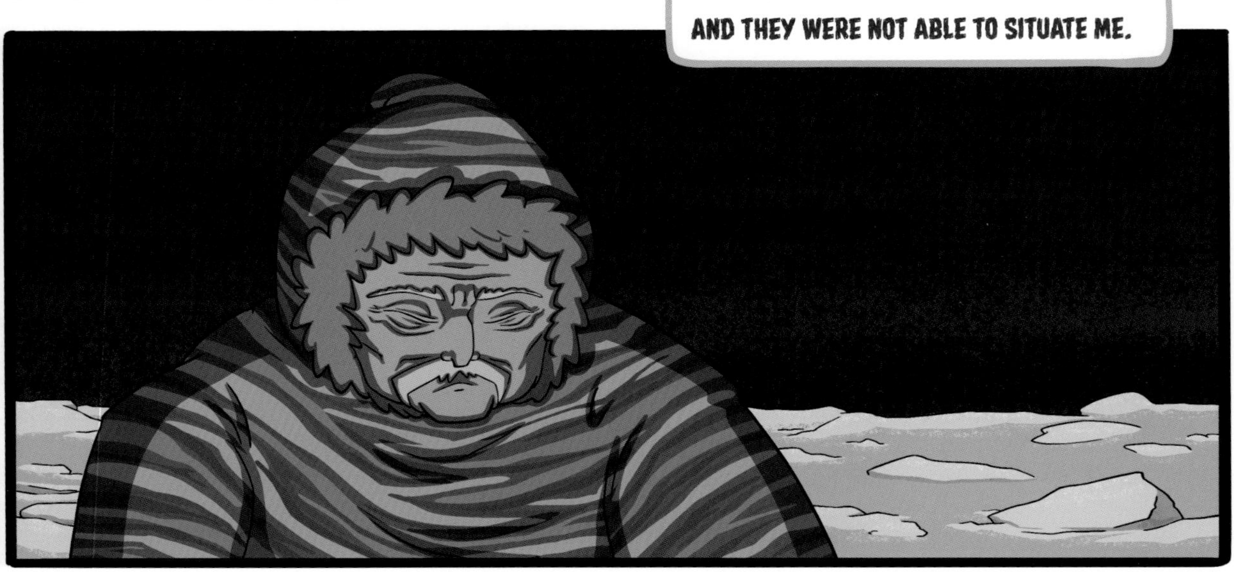

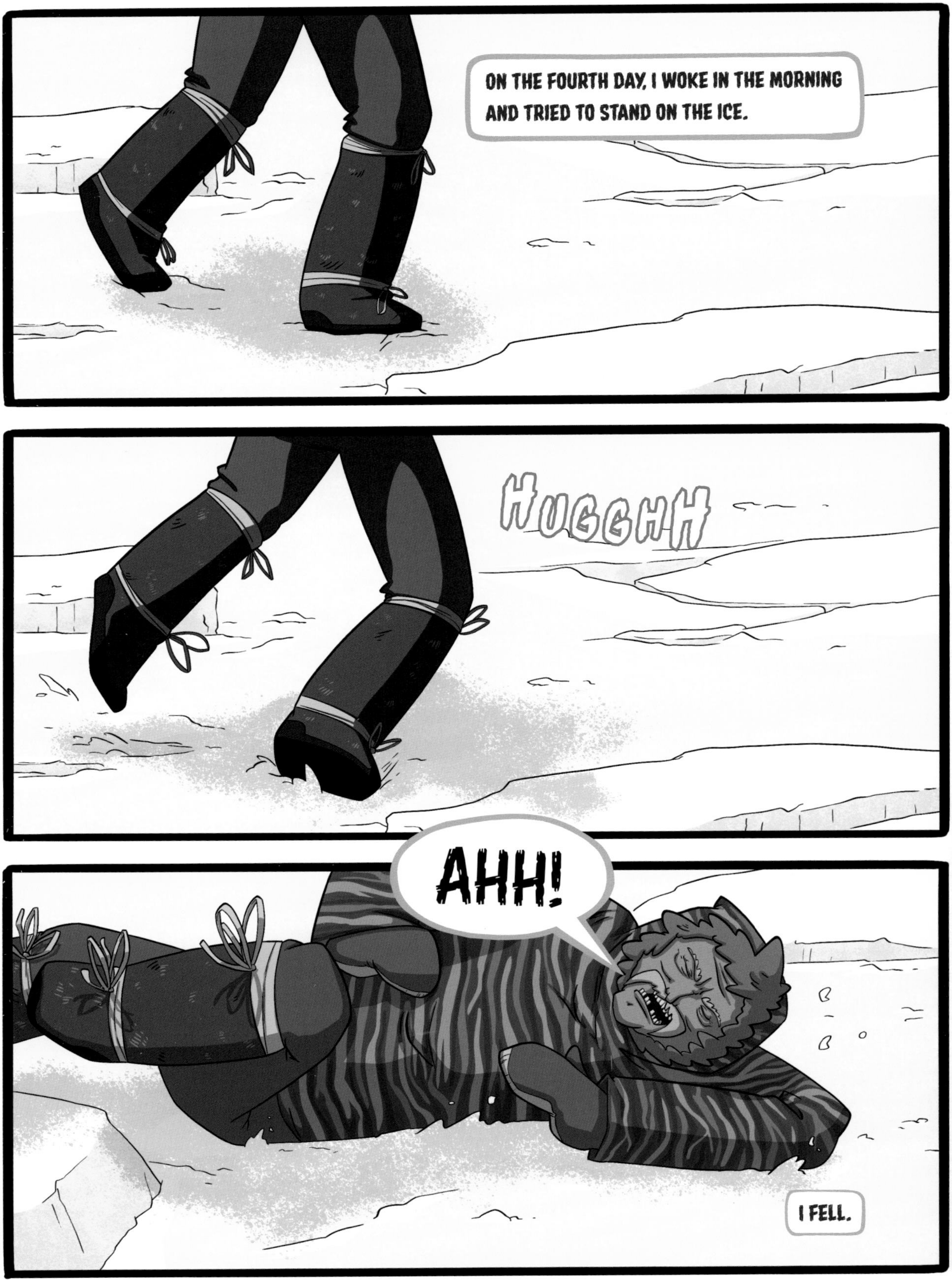
ON THE FOURTH DAY, I WOKE IN THE MORNING AND TRIED TO STAND ON THE ICE.
HUGGHH
AHH!
I FELL.

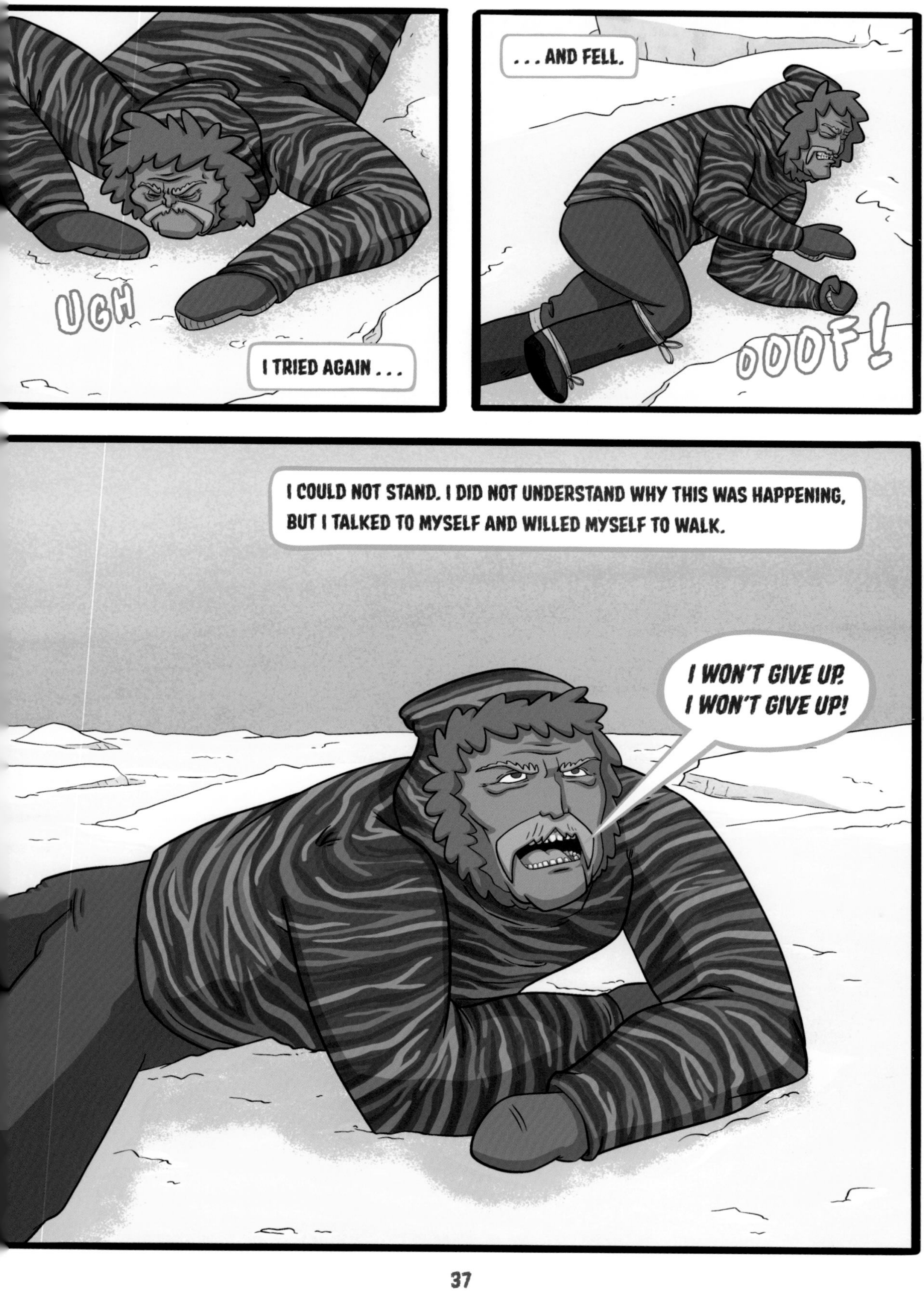
UGH
I TRIED AGAIN . . .
. . . AND FELL.
OOOF!
I COULD NOT STAND. I DID NOT UNDERSTAND WHY THIS WAS HAPPENING, BUT I TALKED TO MYSELF AND WILLED MYSELF TO WALK.
I WON'T GIVE UP. I WON'T GIVE UP!

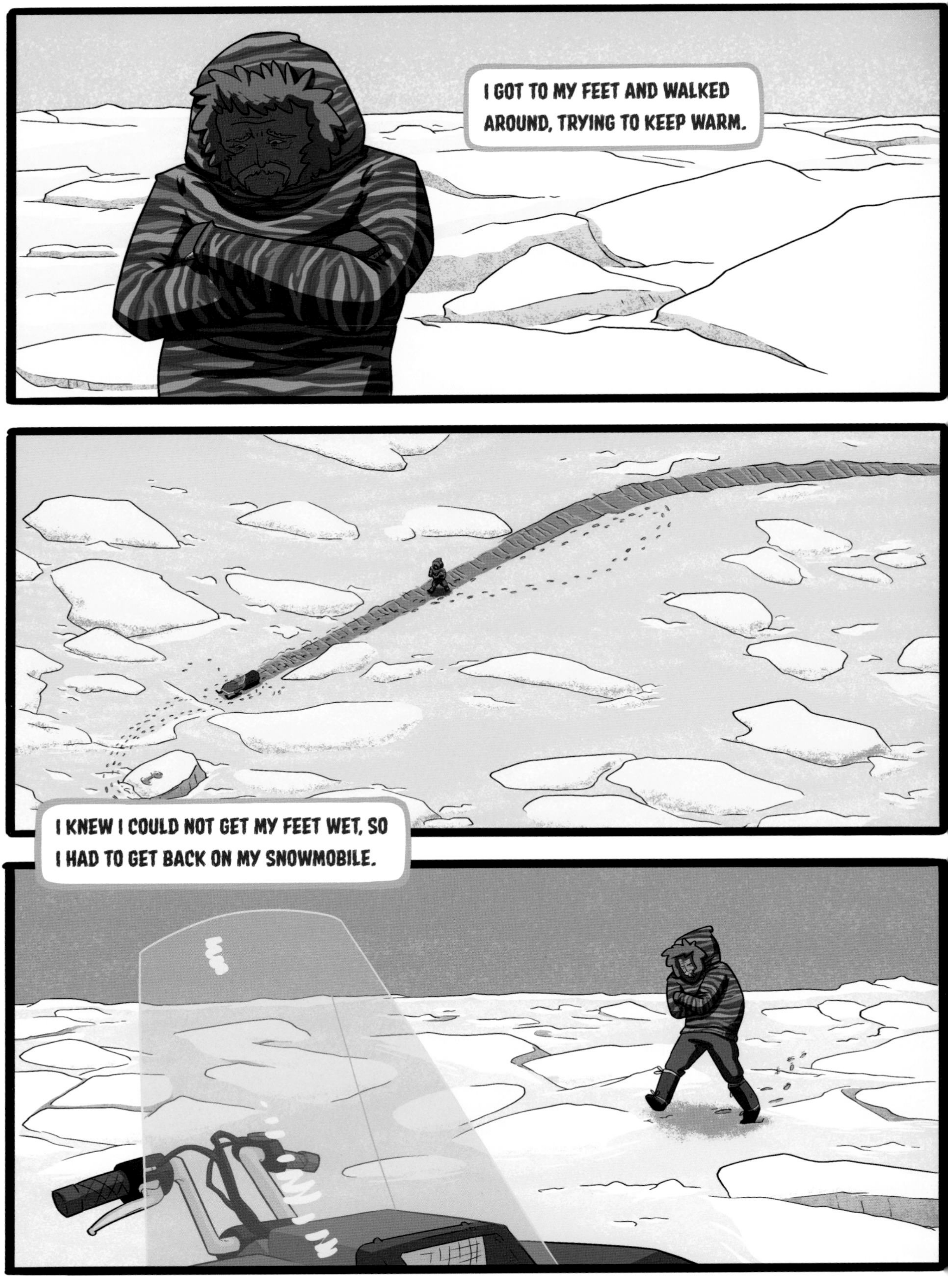
I GOT TO MY FEET AND WALKED AROUND, TRYING TO KEEP WARM.
I KNEW I COULD NOT GET MY FEET WET, SO I HAD TO GET BACK ON MY SNOWMOBILE.

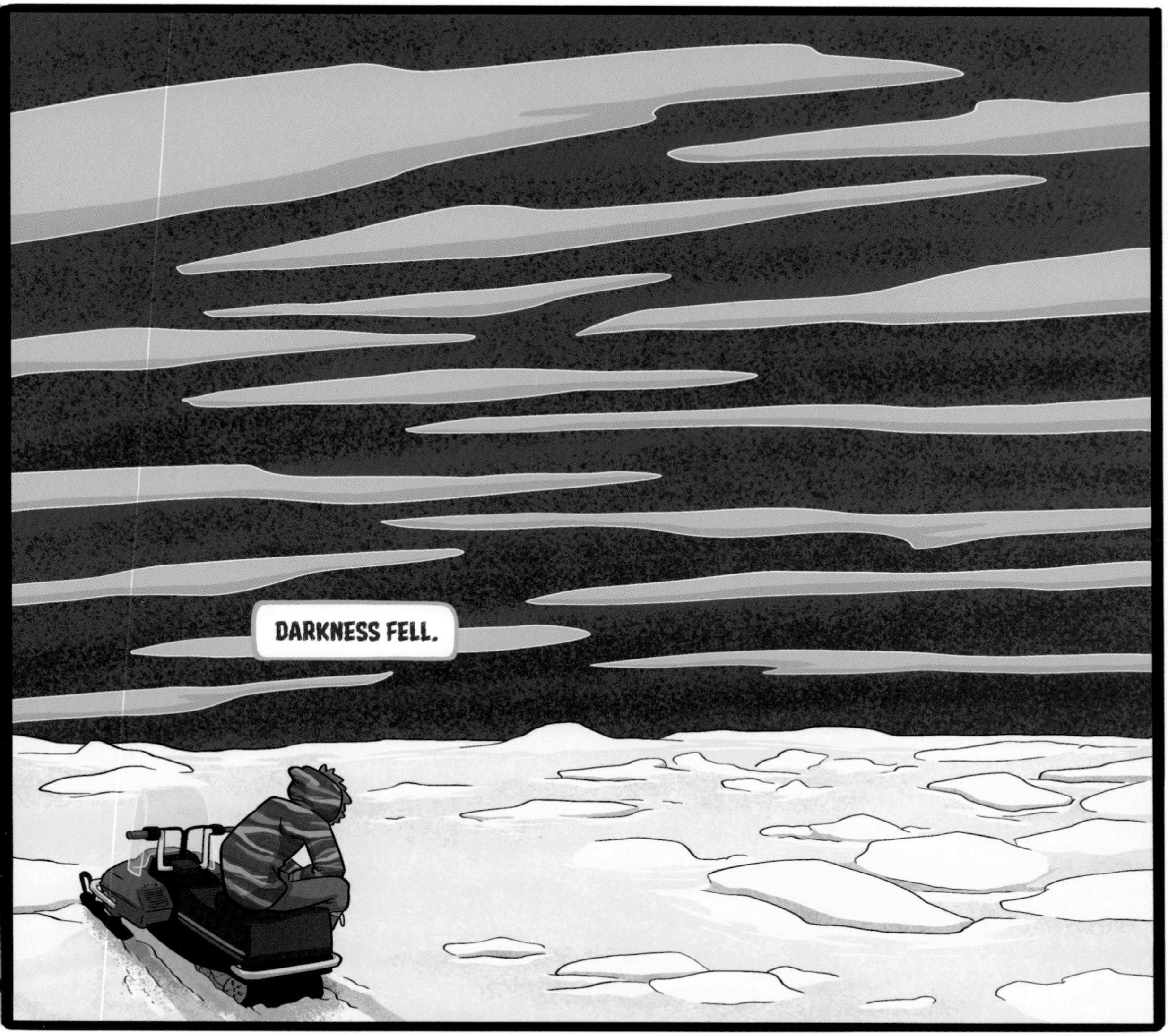
DARKNESS FELL.

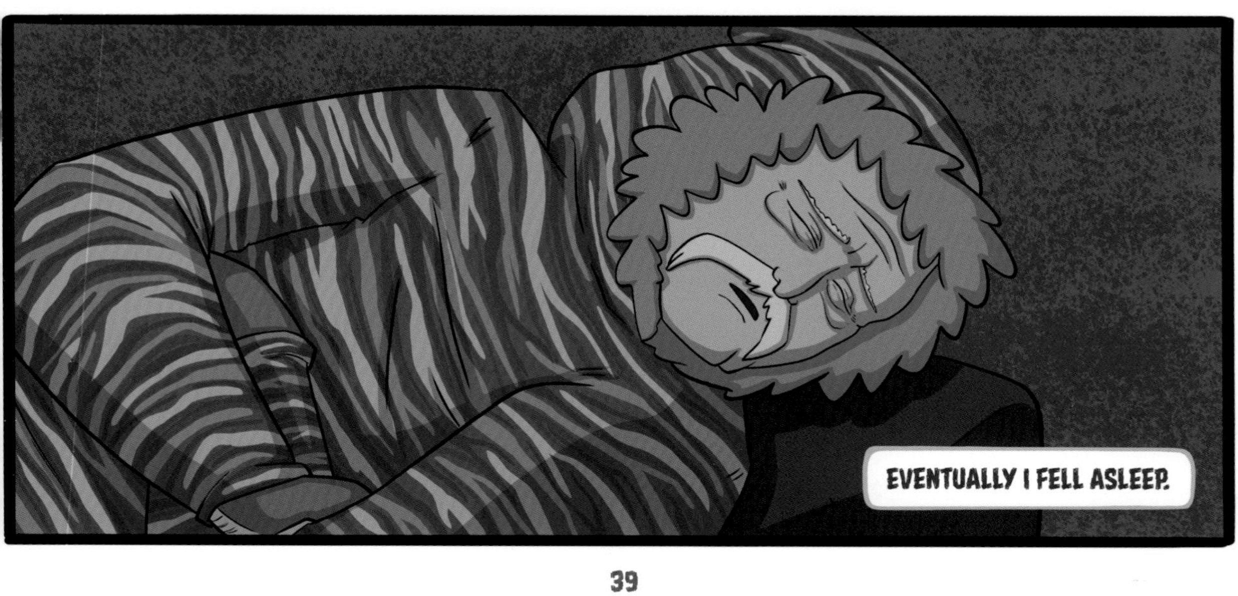
EVENTUALLY I FELL ASLEEP.

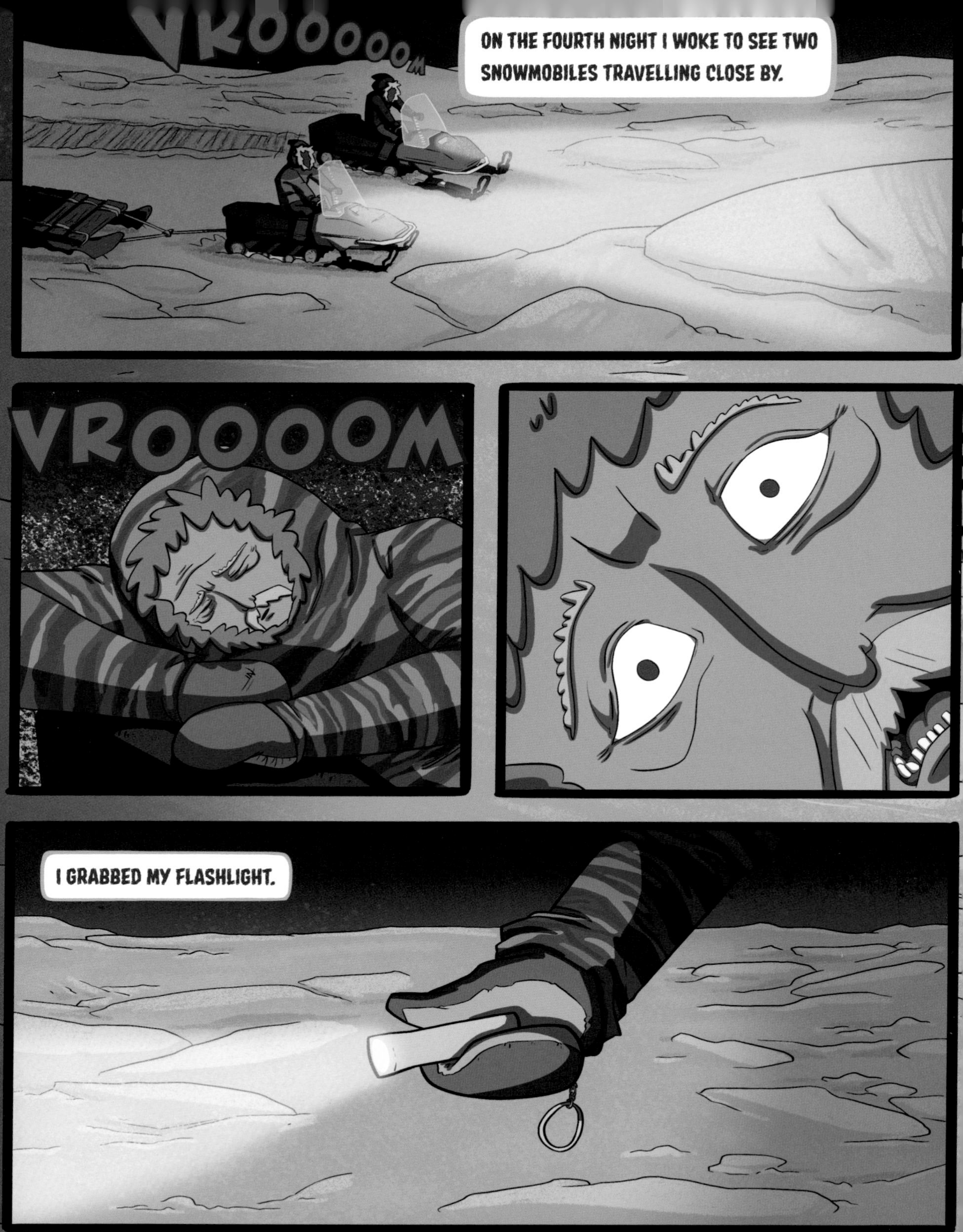
VKOOOOOM
ON THE FOURTH NIGHT I WOKE TO SEE TWO SNOWMOBILES TRAVELLING CLOSE BY.
VROOOOM
I GRABBED MY FLASHLIGHT.

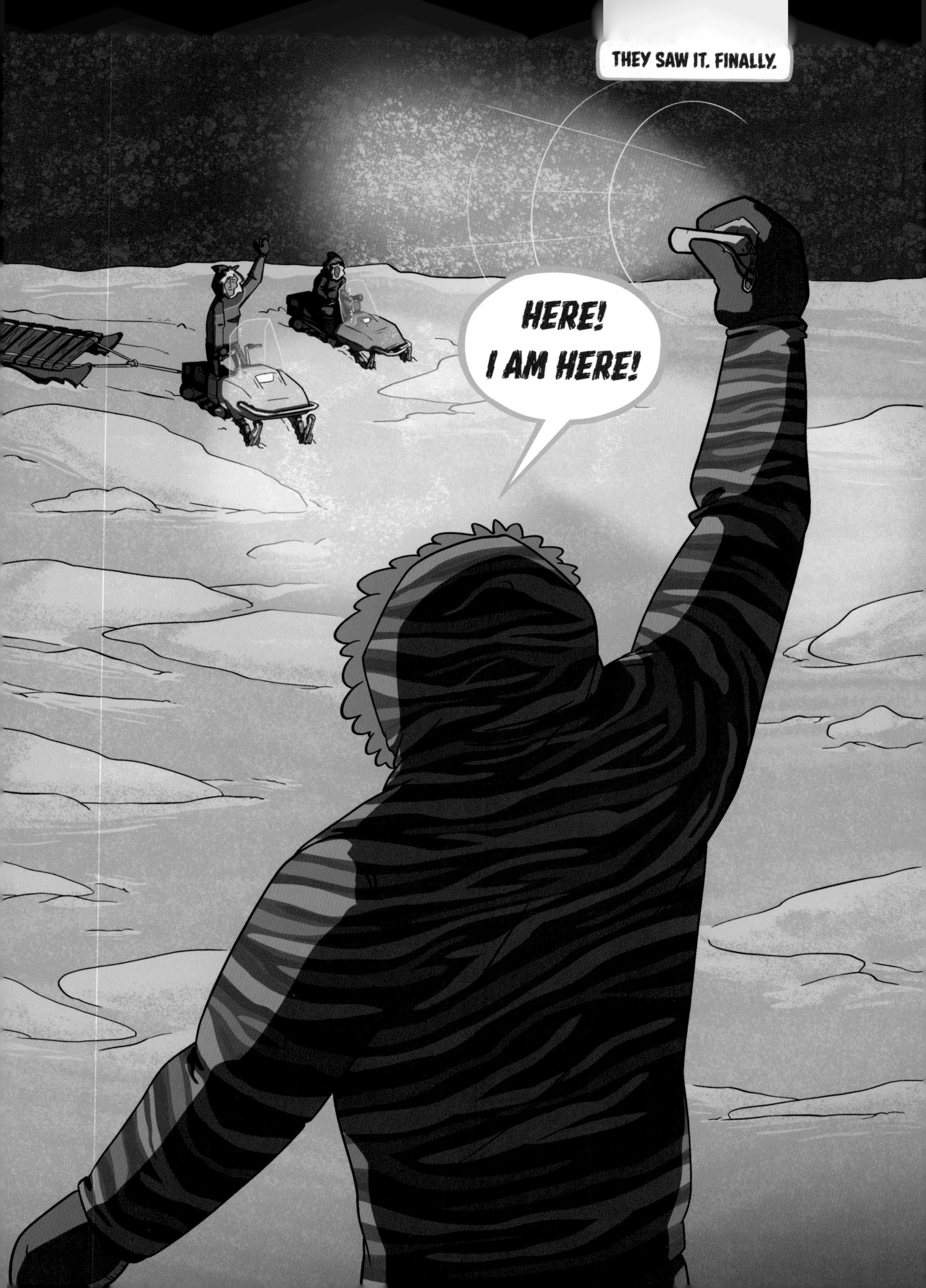
THEY SAW IT. FINALLY.
HERE! I AM HERE!

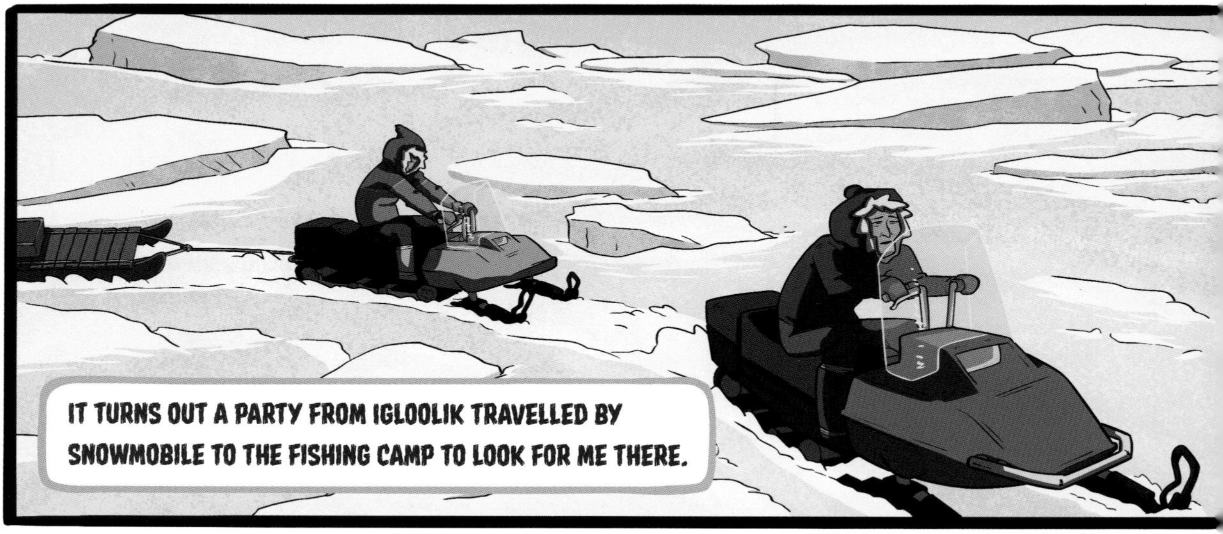
IT TURNS OUT A PARTY FROM IGLOOLIK TRAVELLED BY SNOWMOBILE TO THE FISHING CAMP TO LOOK FOR ME THERE.

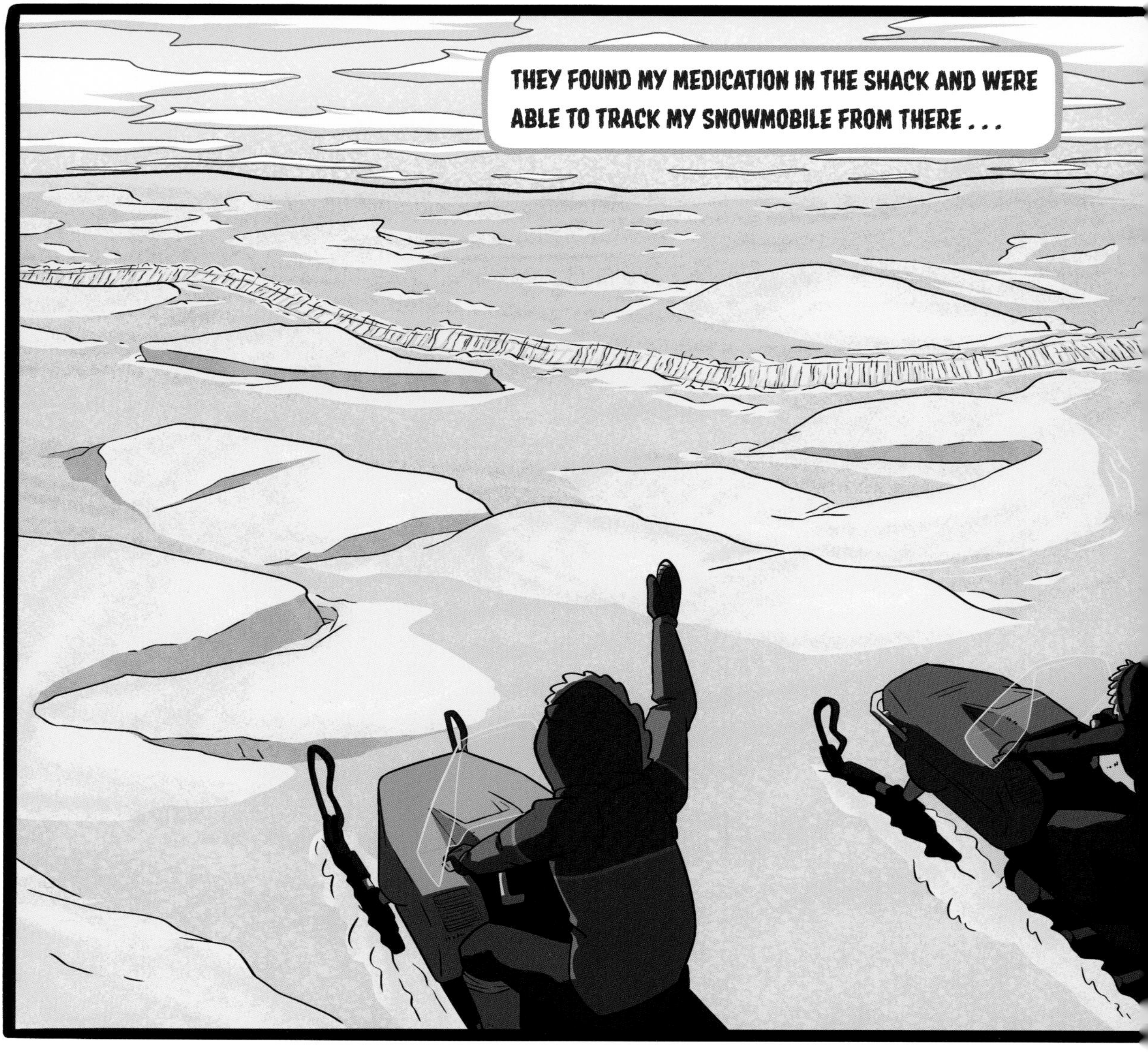
THEY FOUND MY MEDICATION IN THE SHACK AND WERE ABLE TO TRACK MY SNOWMOBILE FROM THERE . . .

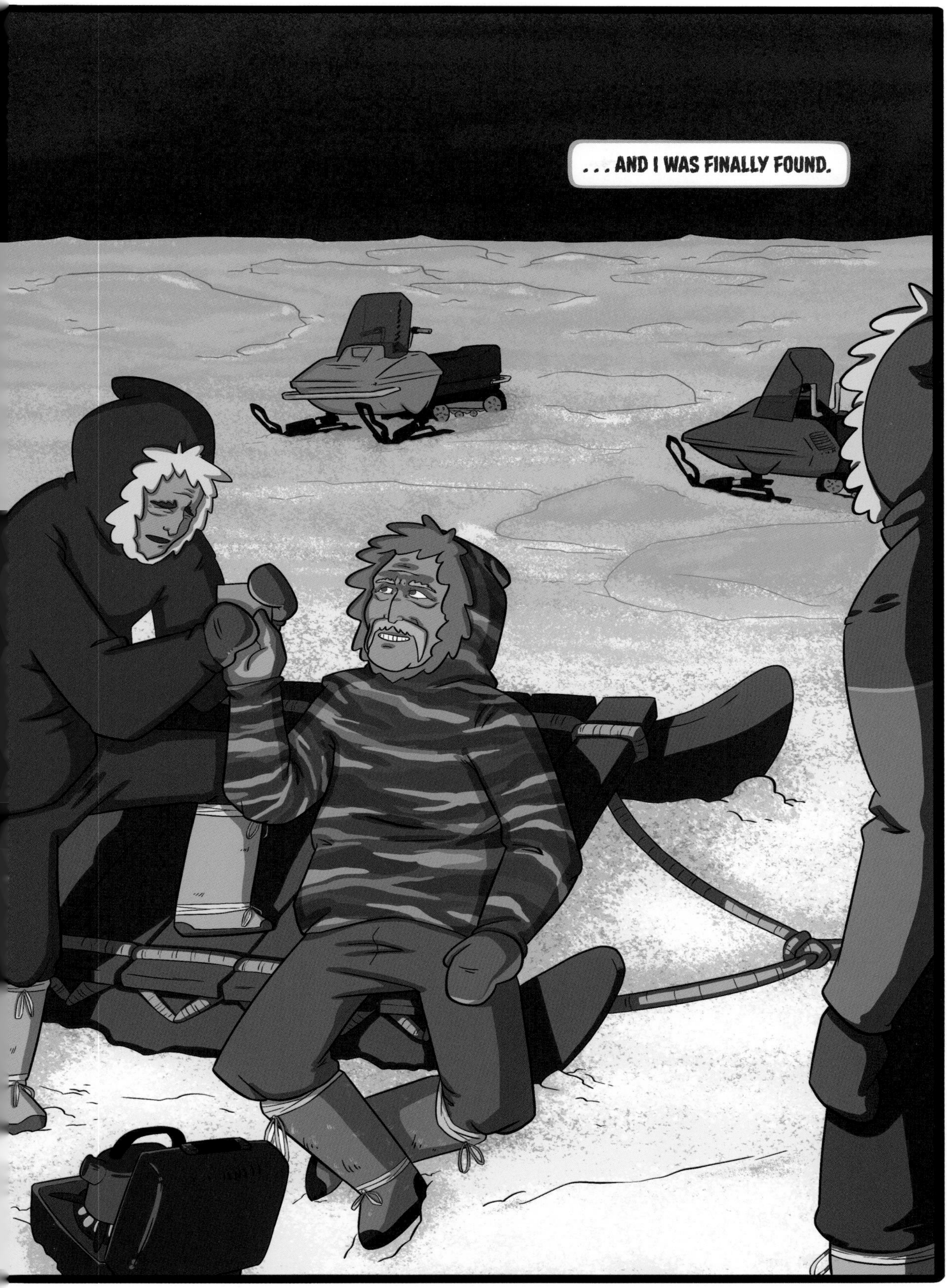
. . . AND I WAS FINALLY FOUND.

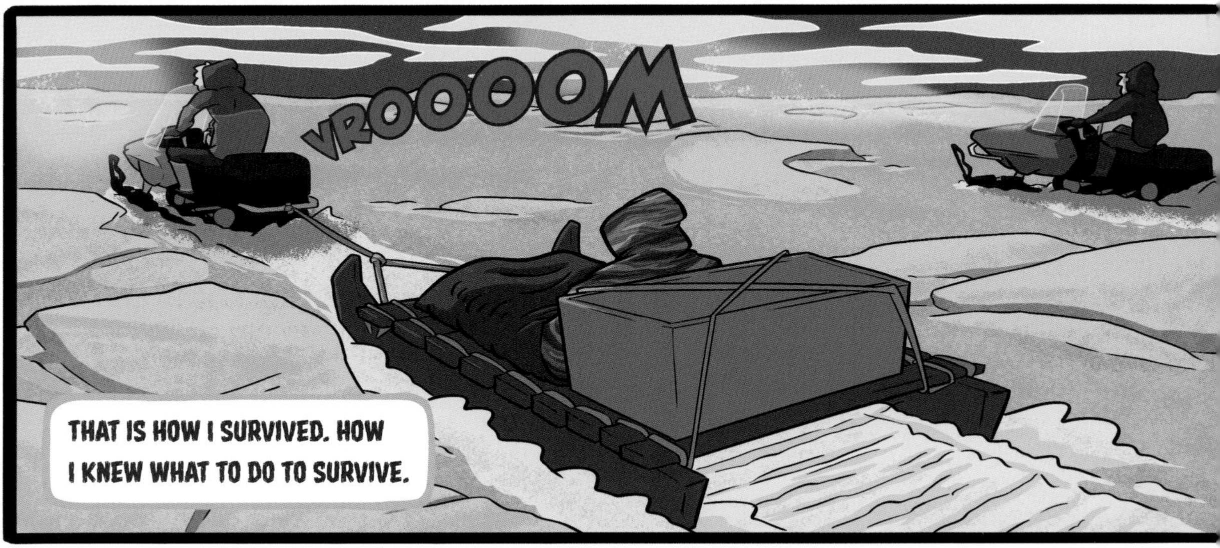
VROOOOOM
THAT IS HOW I SURVIVED. HOW I KNEW WHAT TO DO TO SURVIVE.

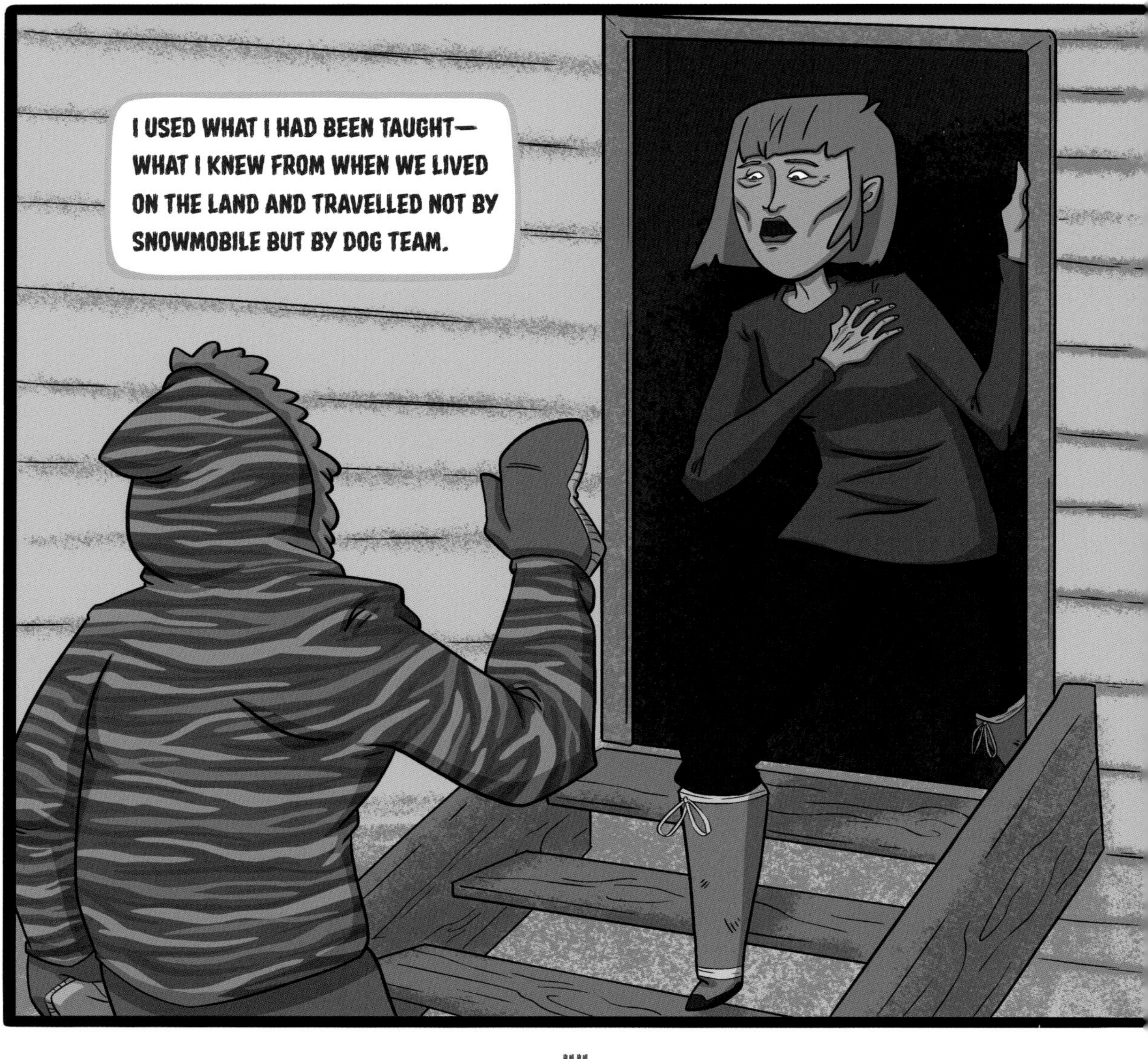
I USED WHAT I HAD BEEN TAUGHT—WHAT I KNEW FROM WHEN WE LIVED ON THE LAND AND TRAVELLED NOT BY SNOWMOBILE BUT BY DOG TEAM.

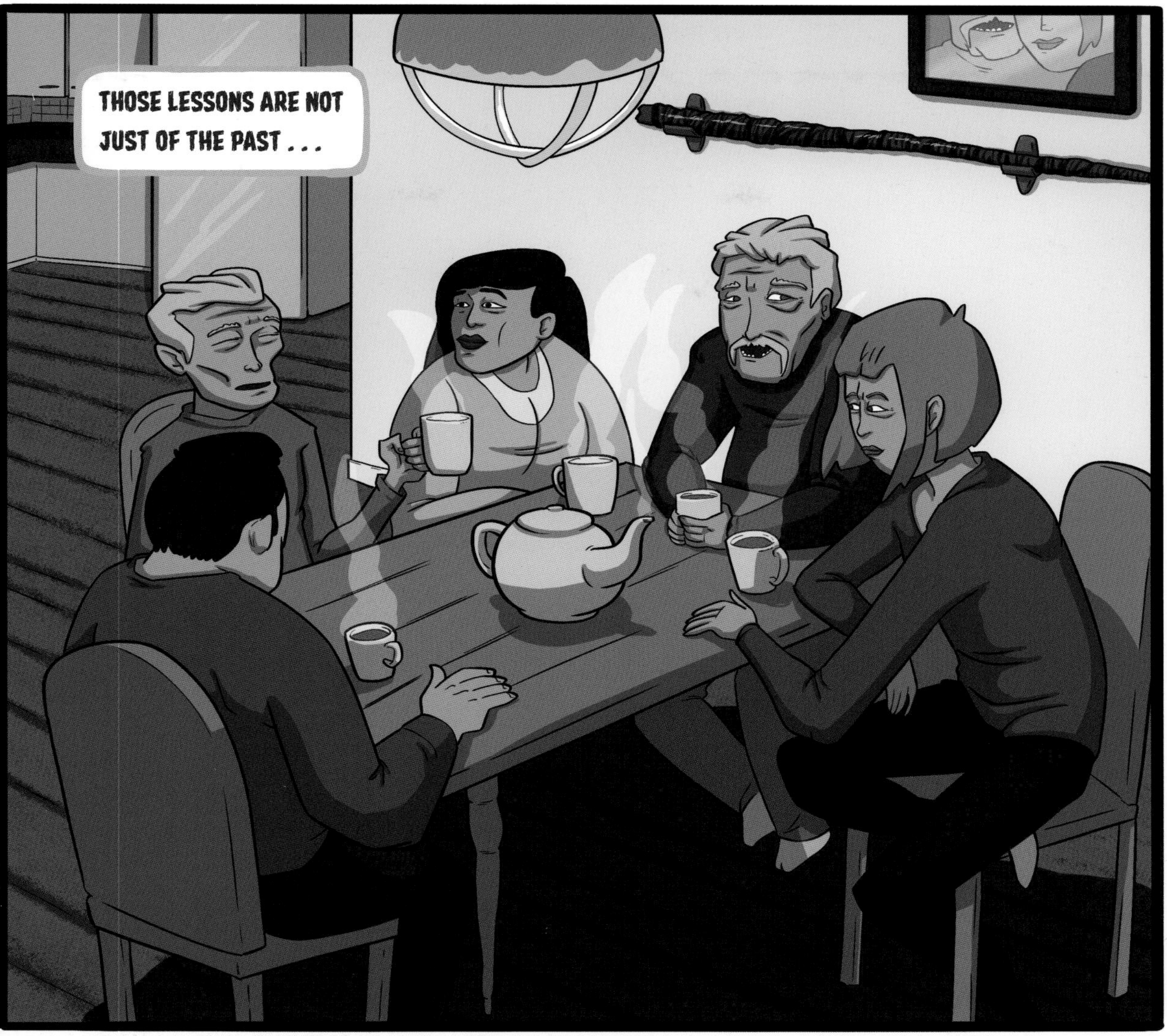
THOSE LESSONS ARE NOT JUST OF THE PAST . . .

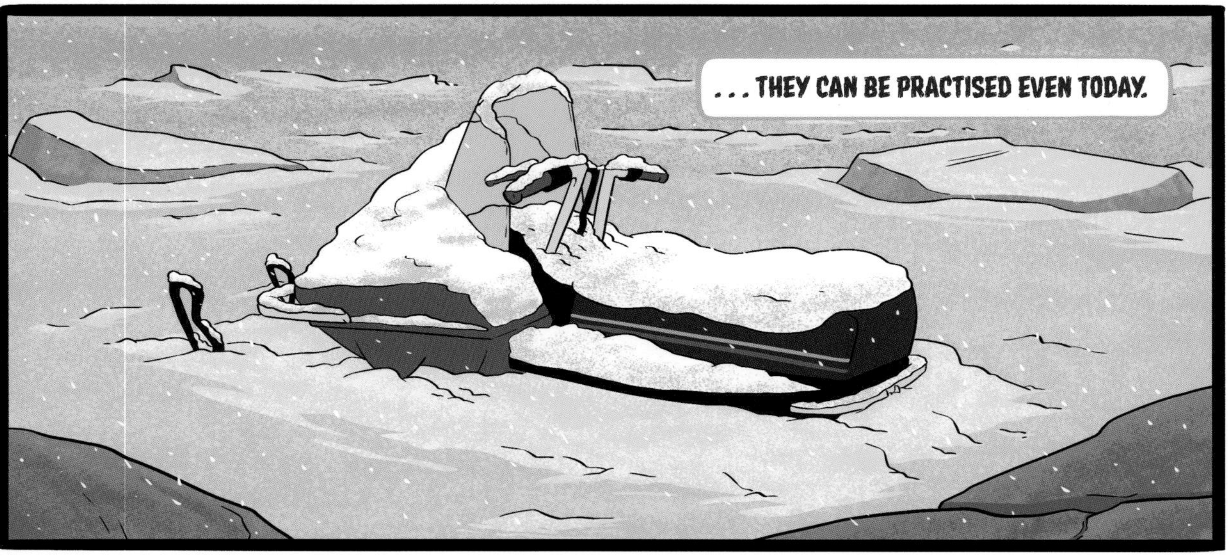
. . . THEY CAN BE PRACTISED EVEN TODAY.

NOTES ON INUKTITUT PRONUNCIATION

THERE ARE SOME SOUNDS IN INUKTITUT THAT MAY BE UNFAMILIAR TO ENGLISH SPEAKERS. THE
PRONUNCIATIONS BELOW CONVEY THOSE SOUNDS IN THE FOLLOWING WAYS:

- A DOUBLE VOWEL (E.G., AA, EE) LENGTHENS THE VOWEL SOUND.
- CAPITALIZED LETTERS DENOTE THE EMPHASIS.
- Q IS A "UVULAR" SOUND, A SOUND THAT COMES FROM THE VERY BACK OF THE THROAT.
  THIS IS DISTINCT FROM THE SOUND FOR K, WHICH IS THE SAME AS A TYPICAL ENGLISH "K"
  SOUND (KNOWN AS A "VELAR" SOUND).

MAKTAAQ	MAK-TAAQ	NARWHAL OR BELUGA SKIN
QAMUTIIK	QA-MU-TEEK	SLED
IGLU	IG-LOO	SNOW HOUSE
KAMIIK	KA-MEEK	A PAIR OF SKIN BOOTS

FOR MORE INUKTITUT LANGUAGE RESOURCES, PLEASE VISIT INHABITMEDIA.COM/INUITNIPINGIT.

CONTRIBUTORS

SERAPIO ITTUSARDJUAT WAS BORN IN A QARMAQ (SOD HOUSE) AT AKUNNIQ (BETWEEN
SANIRAJAK AND IGLOOLIK, NUNAVUT) ON FEBRUARY 1, 1945. HE WENT TO RESIDENTIAL
SCHOOL IN CHESTERFIELD INLET, NUNAVUT, AND FORT CHURCHILL, MANITOBA. HE STUDIED ART,
JEWELLERY MAKING, AND METALWORK AT THE OTTAWA SCHOOL OF ART AND NUNAVUT ARCTIC
COLLEGE, AND WAS A CERTIFIED JOURNEYMAN MECHANIC. SERAPIO CAME FROM A LONG LINE OF
WALRUS HUNTERS. HE ORGANIZED WALRUS HUNTS FROM HIS SUMMER CAMP EVERY YEAR. HE
ALSO WENT CARIBOU HUNTING WITH FAMILY AND FRIENDS.

MATTHEW K. HODDY IS AN ILLUSTRATOR, COMIC BOOK AUTHOR, AND ANIMATOR HAILING
FROM BRISBANE, AUSTRALIA. MATT CAME TO TORONTO IN 2014 ON A WORKING HOLIDAY AND
NEVER LEFT. HIS WORK RANGES FROM MATERIAL FOR CHILDREN TO YOUNG ADULTS, THROUGH TO
AUTOBIOGRAPHICAL AND INTROSPECTIVE WORKS. HE IS CO-CREATOR OF THE SPACE PYRATES AND
SAGA OF METALBEARD COMICS.

TORONTO · IQALUIT